THE GOD WHO CHANGES LIVES
Volume Three

The God Who Changes Lives

Volume Three

Edited by Mark Elsdon-Dew

ALPHA PUBLICATIONS
LONDON

Unless otherwise indicated, biblical quotations are from either
the Good News Version © 1976, Second Edition 1994 by
the American Bible Society; or the New
International Version, © 1973, 1978, 1984 by
the International Bible Society.

ISBN 1 902750 62 4

Cover design by Button Design

Editor's acknowledgements

This book could never have been published without the
support and kindness of all the contributors, who not only
allowed me to interview them at length about their personal
lives, but have checked and re-checked the text. I am
enormously grateful to each of them.

I would like to thank Janet Sebastian and Sally Staples, who
conducted two of the interviews, and also Oliver Ryder
and Sharon Hayles for all their help throughout the process
of producing a final manuscript.

Published by Alpha Publications
Holy Trinity Brompton
Brompton Road, London, SW7 1JA

Contents

'Write down for the coming generation what the Lord has done, so that people not yet born will praise him.'

Psalm 102:18

Alpha

Many of the contributors to this book make particular reference to the Alpha course, a practical introduction to the Christian faith which has had a remarkable impact on many people's lives. The course, which runs on 10 consecutive Wednesday evenings (or mornings) at Holy Trinity Brompton, has proved so popular that it is now running in more than 7,500 other churches across Britain and now, increasingly, around the world.

Foreword

by Sandy Millar
Vicar of Holy Trinity Brompton

It is exciting to welcome you to this third volume of *The God Who Changes Lives*, a series of books which have now had such an impact on tens of thousands of people that God has used the books themselves to change lives.

Many of those who tell their stories in this book describe how attending the Alpha course has been instrumental in their finding faith in Jesus Christ. An Alpha course – the single most effective means of looking into the Christian faith that I know – is almost certainly running somewhere near you.

I know personally many of the individuals whose stories are told in this book – and can vouch for the profound impact their new faith in God has had upon our church.

If reading this book encourages you to explore the Christian faith or strengthen your own faith further; if it helps you to enable your friends to find Christ for themselves; and if it inspires you to get involved even more in the work of the kingdom of God, helping the broken, the poor, the underprivileged, then its publication will have been worthwhile.

Introduction

by Mark Elsdon Dew

Stories about people, or 'human interest stories' as they are sometimes called, fill the pages of popular newspapers and magazines around the world every day. Why? Because there is nothing which attracts our interest like tales of the joys, worries, pains, frustrations and emotions of our fellow human beings.

Meanwhile in recent years, a growing interest in the supernatural accompanied by a search for spiritual meaning has led to a huge upsurge in books and articles about faith and God.

In this book, a wide variety of people bring these two fascinating topics together, by describing how God has had a profound impact on their lives in ways they never imagined possible. Many did not even believe in the existence of such a God, but now say that he has changed their lives in extraordinary and sometimes dramatic ways.

As in the first two volumes of this series, these stories are based on interviews I have conducted for publication in *Focus*, the newspaper of Holy Trinity

Brompton, a large Anglican church in central London which has a growing ministry around the world through the Alpha course.

Those who have followed this series of interviews in the previous volumes of *The God Who Changes Lives* may have noticed that the subject matter has evolved as the impact of Alpha has grown.

While stories in the first volume, and to some extent the second, have included amazing experiences of those who were already Christians, the vast majority of the stories in this volume involve tales of conversion – extraordinary accounts of how those with little or no interest in Christianity have come to have a profound belief and trust in God. That is for the simple reason that these are often the most dramatic and fascinating stories – and I am hearing of them more and more.

The questions I ask when determining whether to include a story remain much the same, however. They are:

1. Is the person telling the story someone whose current lifestyle is such that I can trust their account – and stable enough not to be rocked by the very act of telling their story publicly?
2. Is the story unusual enough, yet real enough, to prompt the reader to accept that something unusual took place which could possibly be put down to the presence of the living God?

As I often say, it is an amazing privilege to be a journalist working for a church where there is such a dependence upon God to do what only he can do.

But there is nothing unique about our church. There are thousands of churches all over the country and around the world where God is to be found working in equally extraordinary ways.

I am grateful to all the contributors who have allowed their stories to be told in this book. For many it has required great courage to allow some of the most intimate parts of their lives to be laid bare in this way.

In Psalm 48, it is written, 'We have heard what God has done, and now we have seen it . . .' It is our prayer that many others, through reading this book, would see for themselves the wonder of what God can do.

1

'I thought, "It's going to take a lot more than prayer to sort out this little number.' "

The story of David and Anne Kennedy

After nearly 20 years of alcoholism, David Kennedy came close to despair when an official medical report required him to stop drinking or lose his City job. Here David and his wife Anne tell the story of how a church group prayed for him on 22 May 1996 – and how the subsequent events have impacted their family since that day.

David's story

My father died when I was six in what was described as a 'shooting accident', although I have since come to accept that it may have been suicide. My mother broke it to me saying, 'He's gone to heaven and you'll see him again there.' That carried me through for a number of years. She brought my sister and me up totally alone and did an amazing job. She wasn't a churchgoer and I don't think she ever took us to a church service, apart from christenings and so on.

My father left a complete mess and there was a lot of financial pressure, but my mother had support from various boyfriends, one of whom eventually became her second husband when I was 13. My stepfather was just amazing. You couldn't have wanted a better stepfather. But my stepfather was posted abroad a lot through his job and, sadly, for whatever reason, my mother ended up drinking more and more. I think it's fair to say that by the end of it all she was an alcoholic.

I was doing OK educationally until I went to Rugby at the age of 13. I don't know why, but I spent my whole time at Rugby rebelling. When I was 17, it was agreed that it would be better for everybody if I left before doing A levels. My mother and stepfather were then living in Naples, and I went out there for a while and did a correspondence course. Then I came back to a crammer college in Godalming to try and pass some A levels. I was living in 'digs' at the home of an aunt and during this time I met Anne. Anne lived around Godalming and tended to go to the same parties. I had actually met her at the age of 15 at one of these parties, but then we sort of grew apart. It was only when I got back to England, when I was 17, that we met up again and became a steady item.

When my mother and stepfather came back from Naples, I moved back home. It was at this stage that I heard I had failed my second A level for the third time. I told my mother and there was an ominous silence. She didn't say anything, she was just so disappointed. There was a copy of *The Times* on the table, so I grabbed it and looked at the jobs column. One of the first ones that sprang out at me read as follows: 'Bright A level educated young man needed for rapidly expanding bank with European interests.' I picked up the phone to the employment agency and said, 'Look, I'm bright and A level educated, but I have just failed my second one for the third time.'

They said, 'Come in and see us.'

My mother bought me a new shirt for the interview and the guy in the employment agency kind of liked me. He told me that they had two vacancies: one for Wells Fargo and one for Merrill Lynch. I knew nothing about either, but vaguely thought Wells Fargo were bandits so I went for the other one. After passing my interview, I started work on the Monday with Merrill Lynch who, as it turned out, was the largest firm of stockbrokers in the world, a huge American company. It was 1972 and I was 20. The futures department, into which I was placed, was a very new venture in those days. It was fast and furious – very adrenalin-inducing – and I loved it.

The growth of the commodity and futures markets was incredible. In 1973/74 we had an inflation epidemic, and the anti-inflation hedge was to buy things like copper, coffee or cocoa. Anybody who knew what the word 'futures' meant suddenly became worth their weight in gold. I changed companies before settling with another American company, Lehman American

Express. I was working there when Anne and I got married in 1976. Although neither Anne nor I were churchgoers, we got married in church in Fittleworth in West Sussex. We chose to get married in church because that's what people did. I was earning a lot of money and we were living in a beautiful house with 13 acres, stables and so on. I had an uneasy relationship with God at that time. The thought of seeing my father again in heaven had sustained me through to my early teens. Then we just grew apart. I didn't see that he had any part to play in my life. There was only one person who looked after me and that was myself.

Our first child Alexandra was born in 1981, and Anne and I decided we would like to have her christened. We thought we would pay a token respect to what we were doing by finding out a bit more about it. Neither of us was confirmed so we thought the least we could do would be to attend confirmation classes. We did that with our local vicar, but sadly the classes had no meaning for either of us. I can remember thinking that anyone who believed in all that Christian stuff – in the face of all the scientific evidence available – needed to have their head examined.

Our second child Ralph was born in 1984. At the time I just didn't appreciate what was involved in bringing up children. It's only when I look back that I can appreciate how much Anne was doing in those days. I was becoming more and more successful in monetary terms, but this was taking its toll. I was drinking more and more. It seemed to be the simplest answer to most things. It reached a point where alcohol was a daily event for me but, apart from Anne, nobody was aware that I had a problem.

It had started off as a bit of a game. Anything my mother drank, I also drank. She would have a double Gin and French and I would have a double Gin and French. We would do it knock for knock. She normally managed her pills and booze quite well, but she died in 1978 at the age of 48. I sort of meandered away from spirits and became a beer drinker. As it progressed, I got on to stronger and stronger beers and in the end I was drinking just high strength lagers all the time. At one particularly bad stage, after one of my job moves, I got on to Scotch and Dry because it did the job a lot quicker. Three doubles of those at lunch plus half a bottle of wine and I could tackle the afternoon.

I was getting more and more frenetic and earning more and more money. I guess my earning started to peak a few years after we had got married and by 1984 I was earning a lot of money. I made several job moves, got caught up in the Big Bang fallout in 1987, and was out of work again. I found another job with an Australian bank, where there was a lot of pressure on me to reach fairly unrealistic goals.

Between 1991–1996 I was working for another company. I went in under one boss, but then another team was brought in under my boss. My new boss and I had an uneasy relationship and he picked up on my drinking. It was blatantly obvious to him that I would go the pub every lunchtime. We would work from 7 or 8am in the morning till 8pm at night quite regularly with no break. I didn't see much of Anne and the children. Not only was I working long hours, but I also had three hours of travelling each day, so during the week family life was pretty much non-existent. My only chance of seeing the children in the week, much to Anne's annoyance, was by making slightly too much noise when I got home so they would wake up.

By the weekends, after the adrenalin had been flowing all week, aided and abetted by alcohol, I would come down to earth with a bang. There was no chance of Anne and I catching up with each other as man and wife. The thought uppermost in my mind was 'What time is it?' and 'When can I get my first drink?' I was very rarely drunk at home. I had it down to a fine art, just keeping myself at a constant buzz level for hours on end. I had bottles out in the woods, in the rafters, in the garage. Anne hated me drinking.

At one stage we had an old Land Rover, which had a big well under the passenger seat for the jack and tools. I took them out and filled it up with a hidden stash of booze. Unfortunately Anne borrowed the Land Rover one day and had a puncture. When a good Samaritan came to her rescue and searched for the jack, Anne was mortified to discover that the seat was just full of beers.

I suppose I became a nightmare to live with. Outwardly to those who knew us, Dave was the life and soul of the party. People would say, 'Maybe he drinks a bit too much, but Anne just nags. He doesn't really have a problem, and her nagging very probably drives him to it.' But at home it was a lot different. She had to wake up to all the hangovers. Towards the end she said the only time she could speak to me was first thing in the morning, when I was lucid and down to earth.

There was no point in talking to me once I'd had a few because I became irrational.

It didn't show at work. Work was exciting and alcohol took a back seat during working hours although, in time, I began to think 'I can't do it unless I've had a couple of beers.' So it was beginning to have an impact. I persuaded myself not to drink before noon and that worked pretty well, although there were occasions when I couldn't be bothered to wait that long, especially at the weekends. I'd quite often pop out at 5pm, have a couple before leaving for home, have some on the train, breeze in through the back door, can in hand, and say, 'I've only had one all day.'

Once my daughter came and visited my office and I took her out to lunch. When we got home, Anne asked her how it went and she just said, 'You'll never guess what, Mummy? Daddy had eleven beers!' It didn't make a lot of difference to the children. They loved me. But alcohol does induce exaggerated mood swings and I could go from over-loving to losing my temper in a big way, making life exceedingly unpleasant for the children and for Anne. There were wounds inflicted then that will take a long time to heal.

Towards the very end it became physically obvious that I was doing a lot of damage to myself. I was being sick the whole time, but I could do that quietly so people wouldn't hear. Every morning I would shake. Sometimes I couldn't even sign my name. I'd go into a local shop, pick up the papers (and normally another few cans), but then I would try to write a cheque and wouldn't even be able to write my name. I would seize up.

At one stage I phoned Alcoholics Anonymous. They started talking to me about a 'superior power', and I knew they were talking about God. I couldn't handle that on top of everything else, so I just put the phone down. Then I talked myself into believing that the best way out of this situation would be for me to continue sliding increasingly rapidly down the slippery slope. I really just wanted to die. I had a decent life insurance to give Anne, a decent lump sum and she could get on with her life.

In April 1996 I was commuting between Haslemere and London. On that day I bumped into a guy called Nick Henderson, whom I'd seen on the train and then met at a recent City event. Nick was the head of the Futures Department at Kleinwort Benson and, being in the same industry, we got talking and arranged to have lunch. Later, over lunch, we talked about stress and how we coped with it. I told him it was easy – I would just have another drink. Then I asked him how he coped with stress. He shocked me when he said, 'I go to church.' Over the lunch I did not paint a good picture of myself, yet at the end, Nick said, 'It sounds like you need a good job. Would you consider joining us?'

I said, 'Yes', and from then on it just happened very, very quickly.

I resigned from my old company and had to take a month's 'gardening leave' at home before starting at the new company – something which is standard policy to make it difficult for employees to take their clients with them.

During our lunch, Nick had said how he had really

struggled with Christianity and that he'd done a thing called an Alpha course. While I was on gardening leave he phoned me up and said, 'Look a new Alpha course starts on Wednesday. Why don't you give it a go?' I thought, 'He's my boss. I can't exactly say, "Yes, please" to the job, but "No, thank you" to the Alpha course.' I told Anne what I was doing and rolled up at Holy Trinity Brompton at 7pm, not knowing what to expect. I walked in with much trepidation, but as the place began to fill up with totally normal looking people, I felt more at home and more relaxed. I became more open and each time I arrived in the following weeks, I felt more and more at home. There was an incredible atmosphere. Almost as soon as you walk through the doors, you're enveloped by this feeling of love.

One of the provisos of taking the new job was that I had to pass a medical. I was in no hurry to take a medical at all, as I knew that it would raise problems on the drink front. I hoped the medical would go away, but on the Friday before I started work they phoned up to say I needed to go in for it. So I did. I started work on the Monday and that morning I received a call from the doctor. He said, 'It's not good news. I am just warning you personally as a matter of courtesy, before I speak to your Personnel department, that in your present state of health there is no way they could employ you.' He told me that in the various liver function tests there's a thing called a Gamma count. A normal reading is around 45 and mine was 525–530. He asked if it could possibly be anything to do with drinking, and I said yes. At that, he told me that I had to stop drinking.

So there I was on the Monday morning, suddenly being told to stop drinking and I didn't want to. Ten minutes later Personnel phoned and they said, 'We've got a problem', to which I just replied, 'Yes.'

On the Tuesday I struggled through and I think I had a couple of drinks, but it was incredibly difficult. I couldn't function properly and I didn't want to give up anyway. Wednesday came along and I was thinking, 'It's Alpha tonight. I'm not sure about that.' I had a few drinks that day and went to Alpha. After the talk, we split into our small groups. My leaders were Mark and Jo Glen. Nicky Gumbel was also in the group. We were talking about what had happened to us over the last few weeks – and I suddenly said, 'I've got to stop drinking. I don't want to. Anyway, I can't.'

Then Nicky said, 'Yes you can. We are sure that you can.'

I said, 'I've been at this for 20 odd years now. I know that I can't.'

So they said they would pray for me. I didn't say it, but I thought, 'Well that's really very nice of you. You're great people, but let's be serious. It's going to take a lot more than prayer to sort out this little number. I appreciate your sentiments, but I think you are wasting your time.'

They prayed for me a very simple, direct prayer, like 'Lord help him to stop drinking.' You could feel how much they wanted it to happen. Then that was it. I got to work the next day and life went on much as normal. When I looked at my watch and it was 1pm, I thought, 'That's odd.' I would normally have started looking forward to my lunchtime drink at 11.30am. But that lunchtime I didn't particularly feel like a drink. 'That's interesting,' I thought. By 6pm, if I hadn't had something at lunchtime, I'd bolt down the pub and make up for lost time. But on this day, I felt no desire to drink at all. I haven't had a drink since that day (apart from one small exception which I will mention).

The desire was just taken away from that moment forward. My addiction just went, leaving no physical side effects at all. My one and only drink was on our twentieth wedding anniversary some weeks later, when Anne and I went out for a meal to a restaurant. She had a small bottle of Champagne and there was an inch left in the bottom, so I put that in a glass and drank a toast to her. We had both eaten exactly the same meal, but when we got home I was as sick as a dog. I felt it was a very strong message from God, which was, 'Look, you're off the hook, but don't mess with it. There is no intermediate ground as far as you're concerned.' That was in the summer of 1996.

Anne's initial reaction to what had happened was anger.

'How could you do this?' she said. 'I have been asking you to do this for the last 20 years and you wouldn't, and suddenly you go to some blinking 'cult' or something and they cure you overnight.' She was very angry about it.

'What's going on?' she asked. 'Are they Church of England?'

Meanwhile I had to go back to the medical people to have another check up. When the doctor saw the results, he was astonished. Things had dramatically improved. To this day I don't fully understand it. What happened to me was so amazing. There was only one place those prayers were going and that was to God. From being mildly interested in Alpha, I began to soak up everything. I was totally receptive. When I told Anne and the children I was going on the Alpha weekend, they fell about laughing. But even by that stage my behaviour pattern was so changed that they knew something was going on. At the weekend, I said the prayer that Nicky mentions at the back of *Why Jesus?*, where you repent of everything that has passed and ask for forgiveness etc.

I guess that was the turning point. If there was a moment where I said, 'Yes, I am now a Christian,' it was probably then. After the Sunday morning session of the weekend, Nick Henderson, my boss, came up and said, 'How are you?' I just couldn't speak. I just broke down in tears for about five minutes or so. It has been an ongoing relationship with God ever since.

By this time, I was worrying, 'What if Anne doesn't take to this? That is going to be a big problem.' A lot of prayer was said for Anne, who I very much wanted to come to the Alpha supper at the end of the course. In the end she and the children all came. I think it was Alexandra who said to Anne after the supper, 'I'll do it if you do it.' So they both came to the Alpha course the following September.

Anne and I agreed that I would just leave her to do it her way and we would go into separate groups. But when she arrived on the first night, she was so over-whelmed by how many people were there, she felt that she needed me to guide her through it. We got home and she was almost angry about the whole thing. There was absolutely nothing that she liked. I prayed a lot. At this time, thoughts of booze were occasionally slipping back in. When they did, I just grabbed a Bible and read it. I did the same when I felt myself losing my temper. On the second week of Alpha, Anne moved into my group and she began to get less prickly and more open minded. Meanwhile, Alexandra took to it like a duck to water. She was in a young group and loved it. She didn't have any problems at all. As the course went on, it became increasingly difficult to get into bed at night. Anne's books began piling up around the bed. But gradually, the more she read about it, the stronger she became in her own faith.

If it hadn't been for the children, I don't think we would have stayed together, but now we are man and wife again. I just wasn't a husband. I neglected Anne emotionally, physically and I abused her emotionally and on occasion, physically. She had to put up with a lot. But the years since 1996 have been just amazing. Initially it was just like a complete honeymoon all over again. But it is different this time. Faith in God has changed her too. I think we are both far more firmly grounded now. I am beginning to find my foundations and for the first time in my life I have been able to open up to things that have been bottled up inside for years.

Although the children have always loved me, if you were to ask them which one they love – Daddy mark One or Daddy mark Two? – I think the answer would most definitely be Daddy mark Two. They both go to church with us. Ralph is part of a Christian home group locally which he loves enormously.

God got me here in the most extraordinary circumstances. I think he looked down and thought, 'That boy is going sadly astray and there's only one thing that's going to grip his imagination enough . . .' He must have intended something for me.

'I used to say, "This is ruining our lives. You've got to stop." '

Anne's story

David and I were childhood sweethearts. We were 15 years old when we met through mutual friends around Guildford. One afternoon we were having tea at his aunt's house and across this really crowded room he said, 'Anne, one day I'm going to marry you.' He was 17 before I saw him again and we started going out together. We both knew at that time that we would end up getting married. My father was a Westminster scholar and he thought religion was just a pile of piffle, and that was how I was brought up. I was a daddy's girl and I really loved him. Although he sent us to a Church of England school, he was always poking fun at Christianity. David's grandfather was a very strong Christian and used to gather all his grandchildren together from time to time and read the Gospels and pray for them. He was on Dunkirk Beach and offered a prayer up to God, saying that if he got all his troops off that beach and safely home, he would devote his life to God – and he did.

We got married and although David always drank too much, I didn't see it as a problem. We often met in pubs with our friends. By the time Alexandra was born when I was 28, I was getting very bored of sitting in the pub watching David and our friends downing eight or nine pints of beer. But it still wasn't a great problem at that stage. I didn't see David much during the week, because of his long hours in the City, but when he came home for some very late suppers I used to think, 'He's drunk a bit too much again'. But I put it to one side. Things then began to get a lot worse because of the job pressure, and we began to row. By the time Ralph was born in 1984 it was a real problem. He would be very aggressive, and I would encourage him to go to sleep after a Saturday afternoon session rather than have a row.

By now we were in a love-hate relationship, but although I had a completely non-religious background, I think God must have given me strength at this difficult time. I didn't live with David before I got married. I wanted to save everything for marriage. In the same way, motherhood was really important to me and I loved the children and they loved their father. That's why we stayed together. As the children grew older, they knew that Daddy drank a bit much, but they didn't appreciate what that meant. He would hide his beer cans in the woods or the Land Rover, and of course I knew. I realised he was an alcoholic fairly soon after Ralph was born, but I spent the following years hiding that from our friends. I knew there was a huge problem, but I wasn't going to let the world know there was a problem. All our friends thought David was a jolly good fellow and that I was a nag. Perhaps I should have kept quiet, but when he was drunk I would tell him so. I could tell by the way he walked into the house whether he had had too much or not. The children witnessed some terrible rows. I used to say, 'This is ruining our lives. You've got to stop.' He would turn around and say it was his only pleasure. 'I'm not going to stop. I enjoy it,' he said.

I don't think David really knew what a happy family life was. His mother was an alcoholic and his father died when he was six. His mother and stepfather rowed a lot. David used to have terrible rows with his mother, shocking rows, where he was told to leave right from his early teens. I knew how a family should be, but ours wasn't. I kept thinking, 'We've got such lovely children, we've got this lovely place.' David knew how much I hated his drinking, so he would try to disguise it from me. When we went out for meals, I'd see him go and chat to the barman who would have a brandy hidden behind a pillar or something. Occasionally I would pour all this out to my mother and father. Once I phoned my father up in the middle of the night when David was getting particularly violent and I said, 'What shall I do?'

He just said, 'Don't worry. I am coming now.'

He was getting quite elderly then and I couldn't ask him to drive in the middle of the night to bail me out. So I said, 'No, it's all right. I'll sort it out. It's absolutely fine.'

It was during the spring of 1996 that I decided I

would definitely stay with David until the children were grown up, but then I would have to do my own thing. I began to wonder, though, if I might start looking around for someone else.

In April of that year, David said he had met this really nice chap on the train who subsequently offered him a new job. David was terribly unhappy in his job, and when the news came through about his new job, we were all so pleased that we ran around the house and cheered. The month he spent at home was a pretty happy month. In fact, it was one of the best months we had had for a long time. But he was still drinking too much. It was then that he started going to Alpha. We listened to one of the talks on tape and laughed at him and teased him. We thought the titles of the talks were terribly funny and that it was absolutely hilarious that Daddy was doing this course.

Then he had his medical for his job. I knew we had been building up to this for years. I was very worried that they wouldn't employ him and that we wouldn't have any money and wouldn't be able to pay our mortgage. I didn't know until a week later that he had stopped drinking. He went off for the Alpha weekend when Alexandra and I were at the South of England Horse Show, where Alexandra was competing. He had a free afternoon on the Saturday and came to see us. I gave him a cuddle and suddenly realised he hadn't been drinking for a whole week. I thought it was probably impossible for him to stop, but something told me – maybe it was God, even though I wasn't a believer then – that it was going to be OK.

Alexandra, Ralph and I came to the Alpha Supper.

David had said that it was really important that we go and meet his friends from his group. I was a bit casual about it and caught a later train than I should have done. We arrived at 8pm at HTB and Nicky Gumbel was waiting for us at the door. I was terribly impressed that he was there and welcomed us and seemed to know who we were, especially as we were very late. He guided us through to where David and his group were sitting and we enjoyed the supper. Alexandra particularly enjoyed talking to some of the younger women in the group. They were chatting about their sixth forms. Ralph was Ralph, just really great. He knew there was a change in his Daddy and was happy to go along with it.

Alexandra spoke to me right across the table with everyone sitting there. 'How about it Mummy? If you do the Alpha course, I'll do it too. Let's do it together.' She was only 15.

So I said, 'OK, we'll do it.'

Nick Henderson kept giving us HTB sermon tapes and others, particularly by J. John, that he thought would be helpful or that we would enjoy. So we spent the summer listening to the tapes in the garden. It was a lovely sunny summer. We would sit on the lawn after lunch and listen to the tapes. Even the children would listen. Alexandra and I thought they were some of the best talks we'd ever heard. David and I began to re-build our relationship. He was beginning to change totally. The drink problem had gone. He still hadn't told me, but I knew that the problem was in the past.

That October we went to Alpha. Alexandra was put into a young people's group. I had asked to be in a separate group to David, so that was all organised as well. But I wasn't prepared for the number of people. When I walked in, I was overwhelmed. Having said to David that I wanted to be in a separate group, I suddenly wanted him to be near. I got really quite cross. He wasn't there for me and I needed him. The group I was in was a really lovely group, but I hated it. It was the last place on earth I wanted to be. I got so cross. We drove home in silence and got ready for bed. I said, 'It's rubbish that course. I'm not going back again.' David was so good. He was so changed by Alpha that he didn't criticise me, didn't answer back, but just smiled at me and went to sleep. He told me afterwards that he prayed for me that week, that I would go back.

I told Alexandra that I had hated the evening, and she just said, 'You're being ridiculous Mummy. It's just because you had to go and do something on your own with lots of people. You're being really stupid.'

She said, 'I managed to go to my group on my own. It wasn't that easy, but I managed it. Go and do it again and grow up.'

I told David that I would go back again, but only on the condition that I could be in his group. So he phoned and organised it. David spent most of the rest of the course with his arm around me. Our marriage was really healed throughout that course. Alpha actually re-built our marriage that autumn. I wasn't sure about the content of the course. Having grown up with my father, who had been derogatory about Christianity for years, I questioned it a lot. I started buying more books, more tapes. I didn't really enjoy the Holy Spirit weekend. I just didn't understand it although I was touched by the most amazing rush of heat through my feet to the top of my head. I stormed off to our bedroom and refused to join in the revue on the Saturday night.

I was even quite appalled at first that David had stopped drinking for God, yet, for 20 years the children and I weren't good enough to stop for. Then I suddenly realised that what had happened to us was a miracle and I was grateful for it. I really enjoyed our small group, led by Pip and Harry Goring. We came up to a few services with the children and really enjoyed them.

I didn't become a Christian until the Christmas holidays, when I sat by our log fire reading Nicky's book *Questions of Life*. When I started re-reading all the talks, I suddenly realised that I was in love with all of it. By then David was a really loving and fantastic husband. He also suddenly started fathering. Throughout our marriage I had to be both father and mother, because David wasn't in a fit state to discipline them. He would either discipline them completely or let them do anything. That caused a lot of arguments and unhappiness.

Christianity has changed our lives completely. I have to be really careful that I don't bore my friends with it! Just occasionally I talk about things that have happened to us here, so that people do know that Christianity has had quite an affect on us. Six months after David had stopped drinking, I went to see our doctor in Petworth with one of the children. I told him that my husband had stopped drinking as a result of prayer at Holy Trinity Brompton. The doctor then gave me a lecture on the percentage of cases which relapse.

He told me to expect it. He said it was very nice of the church to play a part, but that he would probably relapse. He gave me all the statistics, which I took no notice of at all. Now our marriage is how it should have been in the early days. In fact it is better, because there is no drink around.

My faith has been a journey. There have been no dramatic experiences of the Spirit, no dramatic conversion. Instead there has been a journey on which I have fallen in love with the whole thing stage by stage. I wake up in the morning full of joy. I love the Bible and the Christian way of life. My Christianity means an awful lot to me now. I read a lot and David and I discuss what I've read. David doesn't have a lot of time to read. He'll do his morning and evening Bible reading and *Every Day with Jesus* (daily devotional book by Selwyn Hughes), whereas I'll read a related Christian book, or listen to HTB tapes and read the Bible. Now I've reached the stage where our family's relationship with Jesus Christ is really the most important thing for all of us.

We try to go to HTB every other Sunday. Alexandra loves church and would one day like to work for HTB. Ralph is just wonderful. He is what you call obedient. He sees a difference in his Daddy and he loves it. He says, 'Mummy, how can people not believe?'

David and Anne Kennedy remain members of Holy Trinity Brompton, where they have led many Alpha groups. Anne says, 'We now have a marriage based on real love, understanding and family unity. Christianity has enhanced the quality of our lives in every way and I thank God for it daily.'

2

'I sat there thinking, "There is something missing from my life." '

The story of Hélène Murphy

One night in June 1999, medical student Hélène Murphy became strongly aware that something was missing in her life. The answer, she decided, was to 'Feng Shui' her bedroom in the house she shared in South London. But as she moved the furniture, God intervened in an extraordinary way . . .

I was brought up in a Catholic family just outside Liverpool and going to Mass was one of the rules of living at home. When I was 17, I got a job at Manchester Royal Infirmary as a student nurse and moved into the nurses' home there. I didn't attend church at all and moved away from the Christian lifestyle completely. I saw the Christian beliefs as restrictions and thought, 'I don't have to live life like that.' I started a relationship with a fellow student nurse who was a Hindu and that lasted for three years. I qualified as a registered general nurse but then decided to work towards becoming a doctor. I did my A levels in St Helens and then went to medical school at Guys and St Thomas's in London. Once there, I started living with four other students – all guys – in a rented house.

While doing my A levels I had met a Muslim guy at a party and we'd started going out. He was a computer engineer and we got engaged on Valentine's Day 1996 after I had moved to London. We decided that we would marry after I qualified.

One night around this time I went out to dinner with a friend and we got talking about religion. He was a Christian and said that he believed that the only way to heaven was through Jesus Christ. I said that I couldn't see how that could be true. How could all those people living good lives but worshipping other gods be neglected? Anyway, I argued, aren't we all just worshipping the same God but looking at it from a different side of the mountain?

My friend kept saying, 'All I can say to you is that Jesus said "I am the way . . ." ' But I was thinking, 'You are so wrong.' Then I just sounded off with a complete tirade of how Christianity wasn't at all relevant to how life is today. I said the church was very judgmental and if anybody was in trouble the last place they'd think of going to would be a church. I said it was all man-made rules and man-made regulations. Going to a Mass was like going to the theatre with everybody in all those robes. After patiently listening to my tirade, when dinner was over my friend said, 'Just a minute' and went out of the room. He came back with a book called *Questions of Life* and gave it to me, saying, 'You may like to read this.'

I said, 'I don't want it.'

And he said, 'Just take it with you.'

I said, 'No, I am never going to read it.'

He said, 'Just take it with you, you never know. You might be really bored one day.'

I said, 'There is no way on this earth I am ever going to read this book.'

He said, 'Look, just take it with you.'

So in the end I took it, but I was just so angry with him for disagreeing with me. How dare he! I stormed off home and when I got there I threw it into the bookshelf without even looking at it.

Sometime in 1996, my fiancé and I had been going out for two and a half years when he was due to come down to see me in London for the weekend. I'd spoken to him on the Friday lunchtime and everything was fine. By Friday evening he still hadn't arrived and I was becoming concerned. I phoned his house and he wasn't there and then he called and said that the weather was so bad that he had had to turn back and wasn't able to come. So I phoned my mum and said, 'What's the weather doing?'

She said, 'Oh it's fine.' Then I phoned my friend in Birmingham and asked what the weather was doing and she said it was fine. So I was thinking, 'This is just disastrous. He has lied to me but I don't know why.' I knew he had a friend who lived somewhere between Manchester and Birmingham so I phoned her house and as soon as she picked the phone up I said, 'It's Hélène'.

She said, 'He's here.'

She put him on the phone and I said to him, 'Are you coming down here to call it off?' and he just said, 'Yes'. I just knew.

So I just said, 'Well you don't need to bother to come down then.'

And that was that really. I was terribly upset. I continued living in the same six-bedroomed house with the four guys – all of whom are like my brothers. We all get on really really well and it's a really good laugh. We've all got separate groups of friends as well and so sometimes we go out independently with other friends or sometimes we'll all go out together. We all work well together, with very different techniques of working. I tend to work at home and they often go out to the library to work and study. We've all got clinical commitments as well when we are on the wards, in theatres – all that sort of thing.

Then, in June 1999, I happened to have a week in London where I was on my own because my housemates were all doing different things in different places. It was just the way it coincided but I was happy to have the house to myself for a while. I thought I would sort things out a bit and see other friends who aren't medical students. But after a day or two I actually got quite bored in the house on my own. By the Wednesday night, I sat there thinking, 'There is something missing from my life.' I couldn't put my finger on what the problem was. As far as I could see, everything was going really well. My parents are absolutely fantastic, my brother is a great guy and I've got loads of friends. So there wasn't a problem there. I had a house, where I had been living with the same people for a long period of time. Obviously I had got a career that was going places. I was never going to be short of anything I could possibly need really.

I just couldn't understand what was missing and I was really fed up. Then I hit upon a solution. I decided to 'Feng Shui' my room. Feng Shui is that oriental practice of putting furniture and other things in their right places so that the 'vibes' don't interfere with each other in the room. I'd heard about it on the TV and it sounded like a good idea. So next morning I went to W H Smith on the Elephant and Castle and found loads of books about it. I browsed through to see which one would give me the most information for the smallest price and I picked one. I got back and read the book and then decided to change the colour in my room. I had one sort of terracotta-coloured wall with curtains to match and the rest of the room was creamy coloured. I decided to paint it all pale lilac. The book said that it would make it a more calm room – more relaxing and intellectually better. When your mind is relaxed you will be more intellectually stimulated, the book said.

It suggested the bed should be in the corner because the wall would give you security. My bed stuck out into the middle of the room – too much like an island, the book said – so I decided to move that. But moving the bed meant moving other bits of furniture too. The book also said that if you had an alcove bit, which I did because there was a chimney breast in my room, you should put a mirror into it to reflect the light otherwise energy can get trapped in the corners. I remember thinking, 'That's a bit mad' and I didn't do it.

Having read the book, I immediately went to a shop in the Walworth Road and bought my lilac paint and paint brush and a roller. Then I went back and painted my whole room. It took a whole day. After finishing the painting, I started moving all the furniture. It was about nine o'clock in the evening when I decided to move the bookshelves and I was exhausted. I couldn't be bothered to take all the books off the shelves so I thought I would do some nifty manoeuvring with all the books still in it. But as I was moving the shelves across the room, some of them fell out and the one that fell off first was the *Questions of Life* book by Nicky Gumbel which I had been given years previously. It was the first time I'd looked at it since that day and I thought, 'I've not seen that for ages' and slung it on to the bed.

I finished moving the bookshelves and went downstairs to watch TV and have a cup of tea. But there was absolutely nothing on TV and I couldn't be bothered to go and get a video so I thought, 'Well I might as well just read that book and see what's in it.' I went upstairs to get the book and came down to the lounge to read it. It is quite an easy book to read and I was interested in what he had to say about why Jesus died and things like that. I never really understood that despite my Christian upbringing. I read the whole book that night and by the end I was quite emotional. I was quite tearful and I cried – and I didn't know why.

I decided I needed to do something about it, so I phoned Nicky Gumbel's church, Holy Trinity Brompton, the next morning because the number is in the back of the book.

I said, 'My name is Hélène Murphy. I have just read Nicky Gumbel's book *Questions of Life* and I was wondering when you were doing your next Alpha course.' They said, 'The next one starts at the end of September. Would you like to come?' I said yes. This was June and I was quite disappointed when they said September because I was hoping they were going to say there was one starting the next week. So I had to wait. Later I phoned my Mum and told her I was going on a course about Christianity and she nearly passed out. I asked her if she had ever heard of Nicky Gumbel and she said, 'Oh I've just been to a talk of his at a conference.' She had recently been to a Catholic Alpha conference and so knew all about Nicky Gumbel and Alpha, but she was really calm about it all and played it down. She didn't say anything else and never spoke of it again unless I mentioned it.

When I turned up to the first night of Alpha that September, I was so nervous. I thought, 'If I see anybody with a tambourine I am not going to stay; if I see anybody wearing Jesus sandals I'm not staying' and all these mad things. But when I reached the church driveway there was a really handsome man there directing people and I thought, 'Blimey, if they're all like that it will be all right.' I registered my name in the tent and someone then asked another chap to take me to my group. I looked at him and thought, 'That's two handsome men in about 10 minutes. This Christianity is not bad.' I then sat down in my group and had polite chit-chat with people and had supper. Then the guitarist got up and said, 'Well here it is, your worst nightmare: Christians with guitars.' And I thought, 'Oh he can read my mind.' I relaxed a bit after that and I quite liked the singing.

My group were a really nice bunch of people. Then, when Nicky Gumbel stood up to speak, I thought he was really funny and that he spoke really well. When I got home, I was very enthusiastic. In fact when someone asked my flatmate what I'd thought of it, he said, 'Well if you can think of every adjective that means fantastic she has probably used them all tonight!' I loved it and it just got better as it went along. Then my group leader, Julia Mackworth, invited me to a Sunday service. Later on when I got home I became incredibly emotional again with sobs – tears that I couldn't stop. I didn't feel unhappy. It was kind of the same as when I read the book.

That night I thought, 'There is some serious stuff going on here.' I went to bed and decided to pray. I thanked God for all the great things in my life – my family, friends, home, job, and so on – and then started saying sorry for a range of things. I prayed, 'God take my life back. Have control again.' Then, as I was praying, I had this overwhelming feeling of 'Well, you are a Christian. You might as well start telling every-body.' The next day I told my housemates that I had become a Christian and they said, 'Whatever you think is good for you.' I think they might have thought I was a bit mad.

I went to the Alpha weekend in Worthing and on

the Saturday evening they prayed for the Holy Spirit to come and to touch people's lives. This time I was absolutely uncontrollably sobbing. I just couldn't stop crying. I wasn't unhappy at all, but just felt really warm and all that sort of stuff and I couldn't stop crying at all. Julia prayed with me and I can't even remember what she prayed for me but as we were walking out of the room to go for dinner, something hit me like a thunderbolt. I realised I was going to have to organise a complete career change. Up to then, my job plans were always focused on how much money I could get, what kind of a car I could get, how big a house I could buy . . . all that sort of thing. I wanted the kind of career where I could say, 'I am a paediatric cardiac surgeon' or something so that people could say, 'Wow, that's fantastic.' But suddenly all that completely changed. I realised I wanted to stay in general practice and work in inner city London.

Suddenly I got this real sense of vocation to work with homeless people, refugees and alcoholics. Since then so many things have fallen in to my lap about it all. Since finishing Alpha, whenever I was in situations where I would have been worrying about money or accommodation or relationships or parents' health issues, I have prayed about them and felt the weight lifted off my shoulders about them. Although I haven't got all the answers I know that the answers I need will arrive at some stage and I can only do what I am supposed to do. I don't feel the need to have to rush round to try to do everything. It's just like having a friend with you all the time who I can discuss things with.

Before Alpha, Jesus was just this kind of blurred figure. I never really thought of him like a man I could chat to. It is only now that I realise he did die for me, which is just the most amazing thing. Now I read the Bible and pray before I go to sleep. I think having one of those guide books is really helpful to point out what it is trying to say. I found the Nicky Gumbel book *30 Days* really helpful to get me going. I never thought of the Bible as being relevant to me or useful or anything at all – but now I see it as the guide book to my life.

As part of my training, we have what is called an 'elective period' coming up between August and October when students get some more clinical experience with various different organisations. So I just dropped a casual e-mail to a GP co-ordinator in London about my desire to work with the homeless and she e-mailed straight back to say would I like to do a placement for eight weeks at the Hurley Clinic on the South Bank which has got a massive refugee population. To me it was just like a dream come true. I feel so relaxed about the whole situation and I just feel that it's not me that's controlling it all. It is all out of my hands and I am being guided.

I certainly feel differently about Feng Shui now. Now I think that if people are prepared to believe that hanging wood chimes in the doorway can change the direction of their life, why can't they accept that Jesus was a man who died for us and rose from the dead? If proponents of Feng Shui are prepared to go out on a limb for something that has no substance or foundation or proof, how can they disagree with something that has so much evidence?

Before I became a Christian I had this huge hole that I couldn't fill with anything. I didn't know what it was. I couldn't put my finger on it at all. And it didn't matter how full my social life was or how hard I worked or how often I saw my parents or how much I travelled. None of that made any difference to it. It all seemed to be without a point. Now I feel as though everything I do is significant because everything I do affects other people and affects my relationship with God. I really don't feel as if I've got that hole there any more. It has been completely filled up.

Hélène Murphy now attends St Paul's Church, Hammersmith, where she helps on Alpha courses and with the children's work. Her medical training is continuing and she says, 'I am certain, now more than ever, of my vocation to work in the inner city.'

'One night I looked in the mirror – stoned out of my nut and just really pale and skinny – and said to myself, "What are you? Who are you?" '

The story of Ben Hume-Wright

University student Ben Hume-Wright, 22, had lived a lifestyle of drugs and clubbing for six years when his sister invited him on an Alpha course. Here he describes the extraordinary changes in his life:

I'm the youngest of seven children – I've got five sisters and one brother – and we used to go occasionally to the local Catholic church near our home in Fleet, Hampshire. But the church was just dull and part of our Sunday routine. It didn't seem to have anything to offer me. When I was eight, I was sent to boarding school at a place called The Oratory in the Chilterns, near Reading. I got really homesick but it gave me a realistic perception of life, I suppose. When I was 13, I went to a school in Farnborough, near where I lived, called The Salesian. That was a Christian school and lots of the teachers were called 'Brother', but that side of things I considered fairly irrelevant. It was full of people who I didn't really want to associate myself with – either Christian-type people, or very intellectual, or arrogant. I didn't enjoy myself there at all. There were a few of us who used to go for a smoke in the field outside school.

I hated the school so much that I tried to run away. One morning when I was 15, I walked out of the house and instead of going to school I went off into the woods. I was fed up with school, the homework, and the routine of it. My parents had no idea where I was for a while and when I saw my dad later, he went absolutely mad. He said, 'How could you do that? How could you be so selfish?' There was a lot of shouting both ways, and I just left it like that. He had been ill for a while and the next day he went to hospital. Later that week, I sent him a card just to say sorry about all the fighting and that. But I didn't go and see him in hospital.

Soon afterwards, I went away for an army Cadet weekend at a barracks near Gosport. When I came back on the Sunday night, there was no one in the house. Then suddenly lots of my sisters and members of my family came flooding into the house and my mum just came straight out and said, 'Right, Dad's died.' He was 65. I burst into tears with the shock. I felt like it was happening to someone else and afterwards I know I bottled a lot of it up. He was quite a distant father to me. The next day I went to school and then went out in the evening with my friends.

I left The Salesian school after three years when I was 16 and went to a state college in Farnborough to do my A levels in Design and Technology, Psychology and Geography. Although several of my friends at school had smoked pot, I never had. I still kept that boundary. But when I went to college, I just thought, 'Well, OK. Why not?' I just made the decision to do it. At weekends, we got into the habit of going clubbing. We used to drive up to London and go to large clubs that play hard music – techno, trance, drum & bass, that sort of thing. You go to dance. I think I took my first 'pill' when I was about 18 in a club just off the Chelsea Bridge. And after that, that was it: I was on pills. Then, a few weeks after that, I started doing a lot more speed than pills because it would last me the whole night, and you can just dance and dance.

A lot of people think you go to the clubs to pull girls, and that happens as well, but the main point for me was to get off my nut on ecstasy, speed, charlie (cocaine) and whatever you can find there. Ecstasy doesn't last that long – maybe just a couple of hours – and you'll rush maybe a dozen times in that time. With speed it will last for hours, and you'll just dance and dance and dance. It's not such a pure, happy feeling but it lasts much longer. Sometimes when I got home, I'd be absolutely off my nut. My mum saw me but I think she just denied the fact that I was off my head. I'd go upstairs, and I'd grab a pint glass of water and try and sleep, but you never sleep after speed. She'd ask occasionally, 'Do you take drugs?' and I'd say, 'No, of course not. I'd never do that.' And that would be the end of it. She was naive about the whole drugs thing.

For my A-levels I got an A – in Design and Technology – and two Ds because I didn't apply myself to Psychology or Geography. I just lost motivation. They took me three years due to a motorbike accident which left me with a broken leg and a large insurance payout. When I was 19, I left home and went to Kingston University to study Geology. I've no idea why Kingston. I suppose it was because it was near London and I was very into clubbing. I lived in a hall of residence called Clayhill for the first year and it was real party time basically. For the first few weeks I told myself I should care about the course, but after that I decided that the course wasn't for me. I was going to give up anyway, so I just carried on partying because I was having a great time.

I used to deal a lot. I'd buy maybe three ounces of marijuana solid or weed, cut it up, and then sell it on. But I was very generous with my gear and I used to sell it on for only a couple of quid more than I bought it for, so I didn't make much money. I'd wake up and have a smoke, meet up with the others and then have a bit of a smoke. On weekdays, we'd eat and then head up to the bar, and go and get drunk. I remember a time when I was actually really proud that I went out every night. I was always looking for more friends, another girlfriend, a better time, and a better rush. All the time my eyes were focused on something else – wanting more of a rush, to get more stoned, to get more caned, to meet better people to get stoned with. I didn't really pull girls that much – I'm not a supermodel – but yeah, occasionally. Although often you're too drunk to go the whole way. It was always a different girl. Maybe I'd see her for a week or so, but it would be so half-hearted. It was always a case of being with one girl, but looking for another.

I remember being happy at Clayhill, but I also

remember many days when I'd wake up crying, so deeply dissatisfied with my life, and not knowing why. I had no one I could tell about this because I wasn't that close to my friends. We were interested in the same thing, but we were not emotionally close. You don't tell the guys stuff like this. One night I looked in the mirror – stoned out my nut and just really pale and skinny – and said to myself, 'What are you? Who are you?' I felt I was so unattractive and had no confidence. In the summer of 1997, I sat my exams in Geology. The rules say you have to stay for the first half hour so I waited for half an hour, wrote my name, wrote a couple of things, wasted time and then walked out in the second half hour. Few of my tutors knew who I was.

I failed the exams miserably of course. Straight afterwards I told my tutors that I was going to change courses and that's when I landed on Landscape Architecture, because it was a mix between Architecture, Design Technology, and Geography. In the first year of Landscape I was still going out clubbing all the time, and really didn't engage with the course. At that time, we'd go pretty much every Friday – Friday night's a better night to go on. I actually struggled through Landscape but did the bare minimum. There are no exams – it's all coursework and portfolios.

We had started inventing as many different ways of getting as stoned as you could – buckets, waterfalls – devices that you can smoke gear through that makes it a lot stronger. There's different ways of forcing the hot smoke into your lungs so that you can take as much of the gear in as possible. There are different kinds of pipes and cooling systems. I'd get bored in the day.

I'd just invent things to do, watching videos and playing on the Playstation, whatever. It was just a question of lasting until the evening, when we'd get something to eat, and then go out to the bar and get drunk. We started to go to the student bar and the local pub more than going up to town. We took fewer pills, but got drunk more and smoking bongs and that kind of thing. But every Saturday night we'd have a pill night, which was our night, when we'd all get together and drop two or three 'E's – enough to get you sky-high. And we'd just sit and play the Playstation. Most of the time we'd just talk and talk – often about the meaning of life, but there was never any Christian element to it. We'd argue about whether or not there was a God, but I can't remember where the argument went.

Pills make you really emotional, but it's false love. You talk to your mates for hours, saying, 'Yeah, I love you' and you're hugging them – but the next morning you wake up and realise how false it was. I remember thinking, 'What a prat I've been.' There was always the 'come-down' as they call it, which is the time when you don't want to speak to anyone particularly, you feel ill, you can't sleep, and you've got the shakes. Psychologically you're a wreck and that would always be the time when I'd think, 'Why do I bother? There's nothing in this.'

One Saturday night, one of our pill nights, we watched a film called *Event Horizon*. I was off my nut on E and got freaked out big time. I was very susceptible to getting 'the fear' at this time, especially with all the skunk (a hybrid weed) we all smoked. Just walking down the street when you're stoned can give you 'the fear'. In the film, the characters are in a space ship that's been to hell. The imagery is very graphic. It's meant to be just a horror movie, but I couldn't get that film out of my head for weeks. A lot of people got really freaked out by it. Something really kind of messed me up for a while.

Every night I'd turn the TV on. I couldn't go to bed without the TV on. I'd fall asleep with it on. I needed the sound, because I thought I knew that something in the spiritual realm was out to get me. It was very scary. I used to make excuses to stay at the house of some other friends because I didn't want to be alone at that time, fearing that the devil or something would have some kind of spiritual control over me. It sounds crazy but it is true.

Then I started scaling down the amount of drugs I took. I actually got into a couple of projects – still fairly half-hearted, but actually, a good attempt at projects. That was the first time I was actually told I was good at something academically. My tutor said, 'I believe in you. I believe that you can do this. You've just got to set your mind to it.' That's when I started to get good marks in my projects. By September 1998 I was taking drugs less and less.

At the same time, my brother Leo began having real problems and started to insult my mum a lot on the phone. He'd just phone her up at like four in the morning every morning and give her a whole load of swearing and a whole load of abuse about my father dying. She was very, very upset and it really tore her apart. He is very involved in Kung Fu and he really

looked up to his 'master'. My mum always said it was
like a cult.

At the same time, I was quite close to Anitra, one
of my sisters. She was not married and I'd go round to
see her a lot. She had been on drugs but had come off
them and become a Christian. She was very cool about
it and never imposed it on me. I was impressed by her
way of life, that she'd sorted it out so much. She seemed
always happy, always loving. Then one day, she said,
'Why don't you come on Alpha?' and she began talking
about it quite a bit. After that, she asked me quite a
lot, and one time I said, 'OK, I'll come on Alpha.'
The decision seemed strange at first but seemed more
normal as the time came closer and closer to January.

On the first night at Holy Trinity Brompton, I
remember thinking, 'Should I be ducking out now,
before I get wrapped up in this, before I have to stay
here for the whole night?' I stayed because my sister
was there. I didn't expect the others there to be my
kind of people – I thought they'd be studious, square
– a bit nerdy. I know that's a ridiculous preconception
and very cruel but that's how it was. Then I started
talking to the others in my group and found that several
had had similar kinds of experiences. They were all so
accepting, so understanding, even though some of the
others were very naive about the whole thing. I made
a lot of friends the first couple of weeks, and that's
really what kept me going. I thought Nicky was a great
talker and I remember thinking, 'They've really got
someone good here to convince people.'

I started coming up every week by train and after
three or four weeks was beginning to find it all very

relevant. I'd open the Bible at some of the verses about feeling lost and think, 'Wow man, this is crazy. This could be talking about my life.' I looked forward to the Alpha weekend because I'd heard so much about it. We went to Chichester and it was really good. The whole thing was just so easy going, so much fun, I couldn't have been in a better place in the world. It was genuine fun. It wasn't like I was boshing pills. It was proper fun. It was such a relief to enjoy myself and not have to be off my nut. I prayed quite a lot and got so much joy, so much life, out of that weekend. I remember praying, 'I renounce all the stuff that I've done,' although I thought in the back of my mind, 'I'll probably go back to it after the weekend'. Then I said, 'Please forgive me for this way of life I've learned without you. I pray for cleansing.'

The others knew that I wanted to stop all the drugs. I really wanted to live for Jesus and I really sensed that everything was going to be all right. I prayed on the way back, 'Please help me with this. I don't know what to do. I don't know what's going on.' That was the first time I really trusted God. I knew I couldn't be a chameleon – a Christian at church and non-Christian with all my housemates, who had no idea where I had been going on Wednesday nights.

I had just avoided telling them. I'd just said, 'Right, I'm off out. See you later.' Sometimes they'd ask me where I'd been and I'd just say I'd been out, or make up some lie. So I got back to the house and a friend called Ali asked me where I'd been that weekend. I tried to be really casual about it – but I was really nervous – and I said I'd been away for a Christian weekend. And the guy who asked me went, 'What?' I told him again and he goes 'What, for real?' And I was like, 'Well yeah.' And Ali walked through into the living room and everyone else was watching TV.

It was such a relief to be able to tell everyone at the same time. I said I'd just been on this course called an Alpha course, and I'd been doing it for the last few Wednesdays. And everyone seemed a bit stunned. I said I'd been on this weekend and it was a really good laugh, adding, 'It's really Christian and I think I'm going to try and stick with it because it feels like there's a lot of life there' – trying to be very casual about it. I stopped and a couple of people asked questions like, 'What kind of things do you do?' I said, 'Well actually we went to a bar a lot and we just had a really good time. I focused on the things that seemed really worldly, that they could relate to. But I said, 'I think something is really happening in my life. It's really crazy but it's a really good laugh as well.' And it was an amazing relief to get that off my chest. Most of them were like 'Oh right, that's nice', and carried on watching TV. But they were basically pretty shocked, I guess.

From then onwards it seemed that I couldn't go back. It was like a point of no return. From that Sunday I knew I couldn't turn back to drugs. That night, I was passed the reefer [cannabis joint] as usual and I just passed it on. I was hoping that no one would really notice, but I know they noticed. After all, it was quite unusual because I used to deal and brought gear into the house. But I just passed the spliff on, and said, 'No, not tonight. I've got to be up early in the morning. I'm a bit tired.' And thankfully that was left. Then I really realised the stand that God was trying to make in me. He was saying, 'You don't do drugs any more. You've been forgiven. You're cleansed. You're you – not someone who takes drugs any more.' I remember hitting the seventh day on the Sunday night the next week, realising that I hadn't taken any drugs for a whole week. And it was easy. It was crazy.

Then, one by one since then, things started to die away. I gave up smoking cigarettes on the weekend because I remember I was dying for a fag on the Saturday and I just thought, 'No, I've got to stay off this. I've got to leave it, to make a stand.' One Thursday night in July 1999, I went to a church prayer meeting to show God that I wanted to be cleansed from my drinking and sex – and to have that life back in me again. That night, for the first time in ages, I cried. I just burst into tears and I couldn't put my finger on anything. It was just the realisation that the death to that side of me was that easy. This was a massive thing for my life, you know – but God just clicks his fingers and it's done. It's dead and life goes on – a new life. Amazing. I had to leave the room because I couldn't stop crying and Tomi, a friend, was just coming in and said, 'Are you all right?' And I said, 'Yeah, I am. I really am.'

Then I went back in and realised what was happening, that I was actually dying to something – to sexual depravity and getting drunk. At the time, I was working behind the bar on river boats going up and down the Thames – and our drink was free. I used to love vodka and whisky and I remember thinking, 'I don't know if I can give up alcohol.' But after that prayer meeting I gave up alcohol for a while.

My friends can all see a massive change in me, but they don't really understand where the difference has come from, because they don't know Jesus. And I'm not being arrogant or boastful about this change because it's all thanks to Jesus. Now my friends see confidence where there was awkwardness; they see joy where there was seeking; and they see freedom and peace where there was insecurity. They still offer me the reefer, but they're just messing around. I pass it on all the time, and they know that I just don't want it any more. I don't smoke gear, I don't do drugs any more, I didn't touch any alcohol for about five months. I still go clubbing a lot. They probably think that's a bit weird, but they know that I don't need pills any more. I feel that the Holy Spirit does more for me now. I just love break beat, big beat, drum & bass and hard house, and all these things that are so uplifting you just have to dance. I just drink water when I'm there and I have just as much stamina as any one of them, if not more.

Now I have a time of prayer each day. I wake up, and thank God that I'm alive, ask for passion and joy – and then go and have breakfast, have a shower, whatever, and set aside some time. I get up much earlier than I ever used to. I used to get up at 11 or 12, and now perhaps eight in the morning. One of my housemates walked in during one of my quiet times, when I was kneeling down with my hands in the air, and I went, 'Oh sorry mate, just give us 10 minutes.' I read the Bible throughout the day at different points.

I always carry a Bible with me. It's in having more and more of a thirst for Jesus that I've found so much life and satisfaction. And people can see the ease with which I live, the peace, the love, the joy, so Jesus is basically life for me.

Ben Hume-Wright continues to worship at Holy Trinity Brompton where he helps with the youth and student work. He says, 'My relationship with Jesus has grown stronger and stronger.'

3

'My shoulder . . . was completely healed.
Then I thought, "Well, this has got to be
for real." '

The story of Judy Cahusac

> *When her husband died in 1977, Judy Cahusac
> was left with two children under three years old
> and very little money to live on. Thirteen years
> later, by then a successful businesswoman, she was
> persuaded to attend a service at Holy Trinity
> Brompton by her teenaged son Bill . . .*

I wasn't brought up in a Christian family at all. My
father used to go to church, but he always left before
the sermon. He just went for a couple of hymns and
then left. At school we had something called Scripture
but I don't remember learning anything. I came to
London in 1963 after school and did a secretarial

course, but my typing was awful. I went for lots of interviews but couldn't get a job. Then I spotted an advertisement in the *Evening Standard* for a secretarial job in a new nightclub that was starting in Soho. It was called The Establishment and turned out to be a new venture by comedians Peter Cook and Dudley Moore. They interviewed me and I got the job – chiefly, I suspect, because they never asked me if I could type. I was terribly excited.

The Establishment was London's first satirical night-club and was the 'in' place in the Sixties. It lampooned all the people of the day and it was the beginning of the satire movement. I started off as the only employee. I worked from a dressing room at the back which had broken glass in the windows. The artists were always wandering in and practising for their sketches while I was trying to type the letters. It was only some time afterwards that Peter Cook and Dudley Moore dis-covered that their secretary couldn't type. They got a letter back from one person saying, 'Your secretary's typing shows much dash and originality.' Then the club started getting publicity and we had a huge deluge of people wanting membership. It was a really happening place. People used to book up months ahead to get in there and everybody came. Beyond the Fringe – Peter Cook and Dudley Moore's show – was on at the Fortune Theatre and the club typified London in the Sixties. We would have David Frost ringing to ask for a table and I would say, 'No. We are full tonight, David!'

Throughout that time, I was leading a very non-Christian life. I lived in a flat with a whole lot of girls and there were a lot of men around the place. To be young and in London in the Sixties was great. It was minis and wild and anything goes. The club folded a couple of years later. I kept in touch with Peter and Dudley for a while but they went off to New York with Beyond the Fringe and I moved on as well. I had a boyfriend whose mother worked for a recruitment agency, which seemed a good next step to me because you didn't have to type. I got a job with a small company with a staff of around 10 people. While I was working there, I met Christopher, my husband, who was then married and in the process of a divorce. He owned the company. After a couple of years, we started living together and we were married in London in 1969. Four years after that, in 1973, we had Bill. Two years later George was born.

When George was one year old Chris began to develop pains in his chest and back. He also had a bad cough. He didn't feel great but he wasn't in agony. He went to one doctor who told him he had nipped a nerve in his back. Later, he went to another doctor who sent him to have tests done. In the hospital, they discovered his lung was full of fluid, so they kept him in to remove it. I was in the ward with him watching as a doctor removed the fluid from his lung when the consultant came in and asked if he could have a word with me. He took me into another room and said, 'I am afraid your husband is dying. He has got between six months and a year to live.' He said he was sorry but there was nothing he could do. I was dumbstruck. I said, 'Don't tell him,' because I knew that he couldn't cope with it. The business was going through a difficult time and financially things were very difficult.

The doctor said, 'We are not in the business of lying.'

I said, 'Well it is better not to tell him now.'

Then I had to go back and have a conversation with him as if nothing had happened. It was awful. I told a couple of friends but I didn't tell him because he was so worried that the business was going badly and the children were tiny.

Throughout the next few weeks, I was thinking, 'What am I going to do? How am I going to survive?' I also thought, 'How am I going to stop him finding out,' because he was feeling progressively worse. Three months later he had an appointment with the doctor and the consultant broke the news to him. He rang me at work and said, 'They have told me that I have got up to a year to live.' They just told him and then went out to lunch and left him. It was a very difficult time. Nobody said to either of us, 'Do you want to come and talk to us?' or 'Can we help?' There was no support or counselling for me and, worse, nothing for Christopher. He went through what I now have discovered are the fairly classic reactions of not accepting it, being angry and then accepting it.

I worked throughout this time because Christopher had sold the business by now to pay off its debts. We had no money and we had a girl to look after the children. Christopher got worse and worse. He was in and out of hospital quite a lot. As he became more and more ill, he was anxious to stay at home. Fortunately we had medical insurance so we were able to have nurses to care for him. It was awful to watch him deteriorate. Towards the end, I was also very ill. I had quinsy – which is a very rare abscess under your tonsils – and both children had chicken pox.

Although he was first cousin to David Watson [the late evangelist and author], Christopher wasn't a Christian at all.

Then, one day, the doctor came to see him and said to me, 'I think it will be days rather than weeks.' The doctor left and I stayed sitting with Christopher who was sitting in a chair, very drugged up and wearing an oxygen mask. I was holding his hand when suddenly he took the mask off and stood up with a huge effort. Then he said, 'There is someone at the door. Will you let them in?'

I said 'No, darling. It is the night nurse.'

The night nurse had just arrived to relieve the day nurse.

He said, 'No, no. There is someone at the door. Will you let them in?'

Then he just sat down gently and died – totally, totally peacefully. I watched it happen with complete amazement. I didn't know anything then about Jesus's famous words, 'Behold, I stand at the door and knock' but I definitely thought I was witnessing Christopher at the gate of heaven. It was a great comfort to me. He died in 1977 – almost exactly a year after the consultant told me he was going to die. He was 49. I was 33.

At the time, we lived in a rented flat and I had two children under three. Christopher had sold the company. He had borrowed against his life insurance, but I did get a lump sum of £20,000 which was quite a lot more money then. Soon afterwards, the landlord decided to sell the flats to the tenants, so I was able to buy the flat for £20,000 – exactly the amount that I had received from the life insurance. A year later, I was able to sell it for £65,000 which enabled me to buy a house, the one we live in now in Fulham. All the time I was still working for the same company, although we no longer owned it. I had to pay someone to look after my children, but it was the only way I could do it. Quite a lot of my income went on that. It was very unsatisfactory.

Things went all right for a while but I felt that as I was effectively running the company it would be fair if I had a share of the profits. The owner said, 'OK. We will split it 50/50.' This worked quite well until I began to suspect that he was doing better out of the arrangement. I thought: 'I have got two options. I have two small children to support and a business partner who is making money out of me. Either I can stay and put up with it or I can start on my own.' So I decided to start my own business. I just told him I was going.

He said, 'I suppose I ought to tell you to leave immediately.'

And I replied, 'If I were you, I would.'

So after having been there for 20 years, I put all my belongings in a plastic bag and left. It was wonderful because it was just what I had hoped would happen. Everyone said I was terribly brave to start out on my own, but I didn't think of it as being brave until I sat there with two empty books and no business. That was in 1986. I started in a very tiny office just off Hanover Square in Princes Street. It was just two rented rooms. One person who worked with me before came with me. We were lucky because in the late 80s it was quite hard not to make money. Although we couldn't directly approach any of our clients, word got around quite quickly so people were coming to us. Things were good. We specialise in secretarial jobs in the media, television and films. In 1989 we moved to Golden Square, just north of Piccadilly Circus and very much in the centre of the media area. All the time my children were growing up which made me feel bad – worse now that I look back on it – because I could not be with them during the week much.

When Bill was approaching ten, I decided it would be better for the boys to go to boarding school if I could possibly afford it. Bringing up two energetic boys in a house in the middle of London was not easy. There was one school I liked and the headmaster was terribly kind and reduced the fees. He was wonderful to me. In many ways I felt bad sending them to boarding school, but in other ways I did feel that it was the best thing for them. In the holidays we always had a student to help and as I now had my own business, it was easier to take time off. Although it was difficult financially, it worked very well. Time went on and the business went well – until we were hit by the recession in the early 1990s. I had four staff by then and it was tough. Then, in the summer of 1990, something happened which was to change our lives. A family called Barrett moved in two doors away from us.

It was a friendly street and there was a lot of curiosity about these new people moving in, who turned out to be a mother and four very attractive daughters. By now, Bill was sixteen and seemed to be at their front door all the time. 'May I borrow a cup of sugar?' –

anything! He used to come home in the evenings and go into the garden and stretch and jump up and down trying to look over the fence. Then he would say 'I think I am just going to go for a breath of fresh air' – and he would walk up and down outside their house. This happened so often that we came to call them the 'fresh airs'. One Sunday they invited Bill to their church, Holy Trinity Brompton, and he accepted at once. He changed into his school suit and tie and went off. When he came back, he said, 'Mum, it's brilliant. It's really good fun and they have really good music. You should go along. They're nearly all young but a few of them are as old as you.'

Later, Jenny Barrett, the girls' mother, invited me to a barbecue and said, 'Why don't you come to church with us?' It was a Sunday afternoon and so we all went along to the 6.30pm evening service. The thing that impressed me most was the number of young people and the enthusiasm. I also liked the music. Bill became more and more involved with the church and I started going a couple of times a month in the evenings. Jenny would knock on the door and say, 'Do you want to come this evening?' It wasn't a priority. I went to the carol service and the preacher invited members of the congregation to pray a prayer inviting Jesus into their lives. I remember praying the prayer and thinking, 'Well that probably doesn't mean very much.'

Later, I heard an interview with somebody in church who had attended a course called Alpha. The person being interviewed made it sound like good fun so I thought I would go and see what it was like. I went to the first night and really enjoyed it so I started going back. At that time, business was particularly badly hit by the recession and my accountant was telling me to make two members of my staff redundant – but I couldn't because they had been with me for so long and had worked so hard. I mentioned this to my group leader in a chatty way over supper and later, during the small group session, she suggested that we pray for this. I said, 'We can't pray for that. It's about money.' I thought you could only pray for the Queen and peace and that sort of thing. The leader said, 'Of course you can. You are not asking to be rich. You are asking for daily bread and you are also praying for these people.' So we did pray and I was really touched.

The following week, the business got comparatively much, much better. I went back and everyone asked how things were. I said, 'We have had a really good week,' and the leader said, 'There you are! That is an answer to prayer.'

I enjoyed the Alpha Weekend and then, some weeks after that, came the evening on healing. Towards the end of the evening, people began giving these 'words of knowledge' about people who were ill. It was all completely new to me. Then they mentioned an injured right shoulder. As it happened, I had injured my shoulder about two years before and it still wasn't right. I couldn't lift my arm much higher than the horizontal and it didn't have the full range of movement. The moment I heard it, I knew I had to respond. There was no doubt in my mind. When I went forward, two people prayed for it to get better. After a while, they stopped and asked if it was any better. I remember swinging it round and round and being amazed that I could do it. It was completely healed. Then I thought, 'Well this has got to be for real.' That was the moment that Jesus became real to me and I asked him into my life. I remember saying, 'Thank you, Jesus, for healing me and I am sorry I didn't believe all the other things that you were doing. Now I know that you were there and thank you for being so patient.'

I realised that I had been denying Jesus. I thought of all the things that had happened that I had probably thought were coincidences: Christopher's last words, the business turning round, other little things. At this time I was in a long-term relationship. Once I became a Christian, I knew that I had to end this – something that I would have found very difficult even six months before. I discussed it with my Alpha leader, who was very supportive and prayed for me. I was able to finish the relationship in a way that I would not have thought possible and we have been able to remain friends. I finished Alpha and got more and more involved in the church. I asked to help on the next course and then went on to help with about eight or ten on the trot.

Bill, who had also become a Christian, was thrilled to bits. My other son, George, thought we were both mad. He said it was like living in the Vatican! I felt I had so much to learn. I was like blotting paper, longing to catch up on all the years that I had missed out on. I started reading the Bible. It was hard because I had a very busy life and a fairly tight routine. To find time to do that was difficult and I didn't probably do it as often as I should at first.

I now think of Jesus with such love and such com-passion. He represents such all-embracing, unreserved love. I suppose that if you have got children it is easier to understand that type of love. He is always there. I think now that I am happier in this stage of my life than I ever have been.

I wish I had been a Christian when Christopher died. I think I would have coped with it much better. I would have brought the boys up in a much more caring way – and I also would have had prayer support around me. I now think that God has been guiding me through my life without me even knowing it. I have no doubt that Christopher is in heaven – and I am so grateful for those last words of his. And I believe God helped me get away from the business that wasn't working and set up on my own. It was a completely crazy thing to do in retrospect – to walk away from a job that paid me a reasonable salary when I had two small boys completely dependent on me and a mortgage to pay. It could easily have failed. I am quite sure God was there looking after me and protecting the boys. For instance, the fact that the school reduced the fees and helped me to send the boys there. It was an extremely popular school with a very long waiting list and they needn't have done it. There was no doubt that God had a hand in that.

It is like meeting the person who was looking after me all along.

Judy Cahusac is now a member of the church council of Holy Trinity Brompton, where she helps regularly with the Alpha course.

'We were there when he died that afternoon ... When I was on my own I would cry buckets.'

The story of David Heaton-Ellis

Polo school owner David Heaton-Ellis watched his brother Mikie, a racehorse trainer, die of Motor Neurone Disease in 1999. During their last conversation, Mikie asked him, 'When are you going to do an Alpha course?' Out of respect for his brother, David went along...

I used to go to church with my parents when I was young but I never really saw the meaning of going to church. Dad was in the army, so we all marched down to church. I was the youngster in the family. My brother Mikie was 11 years older and my sister Charlotte 10 years older. I went to the Cathedral School in Salisbury where I was in the choir – but only because they got chocolate cake once a week. I enjoyed singing but I wasn't into God at all. Then I went to a school called Milton Abbey, where we had to go to chapel for a 15-minute service every day. I was also confirmed – but only because everyone else was. Early in my time there, when I was 12, I was playing table tennis when my father walked into the room. It was seven o'clock in the middle of the week and I thought, 'Christ, what is Dad doing here? This is not good.' I was taken into the headmaster's study with Dad and he told me that Mikie had had a fall while taking part in a steeplechase at Huntingdon racecourse and he was badly injured.

I stayed at school for another few days before going to visit him in Stoke Mandeville Hospital [the national hospital for spinal injuries], but Mikie wasn't really with it for a month or so. He had broken his back and ended up paralysed from the waist down. He was in Stoke Mandeville for 10 months. It all had a huge effect on me because he was like a hero to me and now he was in a wheelchair. I failed my common entrance really badly because my brain was not together at all. I had started playing polo in my teens because we were all into horses. Dad was Master of the local pack of hounds, Mikie was eventing and Mum gave riding lessons. I used to play polo with the Pony Club.

After leaving school, I was given a polo scholarship to New Zealand and I was set up with a job over there. It was a wonderful opportunity but there weren't huge numbers going for it! After I left school, that was the end of church for me apart from Midnight Mass once a year. I just didn't see the point. I worked in New Zealand for six months and was given a load of horses to 'make them play' – training them up with a stick and a ball and pulling them into the game slowly. When I came back, I worked at Cowdray Park in West Sussex, playing polo, after which I got offered a job in Palm Beach in Florida to train horses to play polo. So I went to Palm Beach instead. I was there for six months, after which I went down to Argentina, where they are the best in the world at polo. There are so many players and so many horses . . . It is just great.

I was playing a lot of polo, working for a very good family where the father was a nine goal handicap and his sons were 10 and 6. The handicapping system starts at minus two, which is what your handicap would be if you were just starting. It then rises to plus 10, of which there are only five or six in the world. The best player in Britain has a handicap of eight, which shows you how good the family I was with in Argentina was.

After my time in Argentina, I went back to Florida where I worked for a vet who was an expert at dealing with horses' legs. So that was great. It was invaluable experience. While I was there, I crashed my employer's car into a canal and had to be pulled out by a motorist who had seen the accident. I had never met him before, but he turned out to be the Captain of the English Polo Team. He took me to his home and gave me supper and got some bandages out, which was exceptionally kind of him. As it happened, he had met Mikie. I got fired the next day by this vet I was working for, which wasn't very good. I'd just written off his car and so he wasn't very happy. There was about £1,000 worth of damage, even though it was insured. I think he was just probably looking for the excuse to get rid of me.

Anyway, the Captain of the English Polo team then offered me a job in England, helping to run his stables down in Midhurst in Sussex. So all my experience was coming together – and running the Captain of the English Polo Team's stables was quite a thing. Through that I met everyone – the whole English team, of course, and all the professionals. I got into that whole crowd. But after a while, I left because I realised I was all horses and polo and nothing else at all. So I decided to start a number of businesses. I started one with a French friend selling parts for cars and at the same time sold water filters for another company. Then I got offered the franchise with Sky Television, in charge of selling dishes in the area south of the river in London. I had 20 guys working for me doing that. I also set up a company doing leaflet distribution. I used to go to about five or six different restaurants in the local area and distributed leaflets for them. I had an office in Chelsea Harbour because we thought the image was quite important – and it worked really well. We were also selling hot dog machines.

I did really well out of all this financially but I got bored with it. I thought 'there's more to life'. I sold up the companies at quite a good profit and then I got a call from a friend of mine giving me the opportunity to start off a polo club and a polo school in Henley, Berkshire. It was 1992 then and I was 23. So I moved to Henley and set up the polo school and a polo club. I ran all the horses and did lots of teaching. I hadn't felt fulfilled in London and I wanted to get back into horses and do something I really enjoyed doing. Three years later we had 60 members of the polo club and a business that was just flying. But I had a few problems with the guy I worked for and I didn't feel particularly appreciated. I worked very hard and I wasn't very good at delegating.

Then I went on a stag do. One of my good friends was getting married and I got talking to this friend of mine who was there. He said, 'We need a new polo manager of our club.'

And I said, 'Really?'

He said, 'Where can I find someone to do the job?'

I said, 'Well you can have me because I'm not happy.' If I'm not happy in my work, I know I won't do the job properly. So I became manager of the polo club at Kirtlington in Oxford which was a fantastic job. It was a really well known club with 20 members. Alongside that job, I set up my own private polo school with a partner – my girlfriend – and did that for about five years or so. My girlfriend and I were living together but, sadly, the two of us had rather a bust up early in 1999 so I moved to a really great place down the road and started a new school. It was an old equestrian centre that had lost a heap of money, but now we've got a polo field and an indoor arena.

There are now 120 members of the polo club, so it's really flying. I have a few other businesses on the go as well, including a polo holidays company based in Argentina and a new business in the Caribbean where I have discovered a small polo club in a lovely resort in the Dominican Republic, so I am arranging holidays there. I thought it was another good excuse to go and look at the Caribbean!

Through all this time, Mikie had become a Christian, but I was rushing around like a headless chicken and I thought that I hadn't got time for it. I noticed a huge change in Mikie, though. He was always very good to me but he was quite a hard person. He argued a hell of a lot and in business he was as hard as nails and quite selfish. Then I don't know what happened to him but his Christian faith took over and he became a different person, a lot happier. He said he had found what he was looking for. Mikie never rammed it down my throat, but he did used to say, 'You've got to do an Alpha course. You've got to go and have a look at it.'

In September 1997, Mikie was diagnosed as having Motor Neurone Disease, although he didn't tell anybody. He thought we would all worry too much. But I started to notice that he wasn't as fit as usual, so I went and asked him, 'Mikie, there is something wrong here isn't there?'

And he said, 'Yes, there is.'

He told me he had Motor Neurone Disease and had only a few years to live. I thought there was nothing worse, but I didn't show it. I was great when I was with Mikie and I wasn't when I wasn't. As I drove away, I was just so unhappy. After that, we had an agreement that I would never ask him as long as he told me things. So we did talk about it occasionally but it used to be just Mikie saying, 'This, this and this have happened and I've been to the doctor this week and I've done that, that and that. OK? Fine.'

End of conversation.

Then it was, 'Let's go racing or whatever, but let's not talk about it.'

After he got Motor Neurone Disease, he became even more amazing. He said he may be in a wheelchair with two years to live, but he had never been happier. And he meant it. Then, one day in 1999, I knew something was badly wrong, so I called Mikie. I hadn't spoken to him for a couple of days but I had a feeling something wasn't good. I spoke to one of his carers and learned he was just going into hospital. I went along to the hospital, Princess Margaret's, and found he hadn't told Mum or Dad he was there because he didn't want to worry them. I found him lying in bed with a mask on. He couldn't breathe properly because he had bronchitis and because of his Motor Neurone Disease, he couldn't get the phlegm up and so it was difficult to breathe. As I sat there, he asked me two questions. First, he said, 'What's happening in the cricket?' England were playing New Zealand and we'd been absolutely whipped but I said to Mikie, 'It's not looking good!' Secondly, he said, 'When are you going to go on the Alpha course?'

I had almost gone on one the previous September, but Wednesday night – the night of the course – was a big night for business, so I hadn't gone on it. So I said to Mikie, 'I'll do it this September.' As I was leaving the hospital, I saw a stunning girl walking towards me and I thought, 'Hello, who's this?' I walked up to her and she said, 'Hello David.' I couldn't believe it! It was a doctor and she was my first ever girlfriend.

She said, 'You're not going to believe it but I'm going to look after your brother tonight.'

I said, 'Fantastic!'

So I took her in to see Mikie and I said to him, 'Here we go! Your brother's brought you a fine looking lady and she's going to look after you tonight!'

And he smiled and said like 'Yeah, thank you very much!'

Then I got my car and drove back to my home, which is about an hour away. But just minutes after I arrived, the phone went. It was Fiona, my ex-girlfriend, calling from the hospital.

She said, 'I think you had better get back here now. And can you call your parents and all your family because Mikie might not make it through the night.'

Since I had left, he had gone seriously downhill. So we all came back to hospital and I met Mum and Dad there. Mikie knew we were there because his eyes were open. He wasn't in a coma or anything and he was still ordering us around as he always did! I spent the whole night there and then I was having a little kip in the car at about 12 o'clock the next day when someone came knocking on the door and said 'You'd better come up'.

Mikie was fighting to keep himself awake, but he was quite alert. He was happy and joking up until the last minute. He kept everyone going. We were there when he died that afternoon. It was devastating for all of us. My way of dealing with it was to get back to the polo school and keep on working. But when I was on my own I would cry buckets. Having promised Mikie I would do Alpha, I wasn't sure whether to do it locally in Oxford or to go to HTB in London.

Then I met Nicky Gumbel at my brother's memorial service at HTB and decided to go to London once a week. I confess I was not looking forward to it. I was expecting 'happy clappy' sort of people and kept thinking, 'Do I really want to do this?' I didn't go the first week because it was the end of the polo season but a friend of mine called Dick and his girlfriend Debbie had decided to do the course with me so I couldn't let them down the second week. I quite enjoyed the evening and I thought at the end, 'Yes, I'm definitely going to go next week.' The next week was tremendous. My group leaders, James and Julia Thomas, led the group really well and were very welcoming. For me, the course just got better and better.

The turning point was the weekend. I hadn't been looking forward to it and had been thinking, 'Oh my God, what is going to happen here?'

It was held in Chichester and on the Saturday afternoon a group of us including James and Julia and Nicky Gumbel went for this incredible walk down the beach. It was during the finals of the rugby world cup – Australia vs South Africa – but instead of watching, we walked and talked for about two hours talking about life in general and God and everything else. Later that afternoon, Nicky gave a talk about the Holy Spirit and then he asked for the Holy Spirit to come. At that moment, I was totally overcome by something. I wasn't sure what it was but obviously it was the Holy Spirit. I have never laughed and cried at the same time like that in my life before. It was a great experience – not a bad one at all – and I just kept thinking of Mikie.

Since then, I feel I have a relationship with God which I never had before. I realise that the way I've been living life has been pretty shallow but now things are different. I now have a different perception of life. I think Mikie will be laughing his head off at what has happened to me. I often think of him. I can now begin to understand why Mikie went through what he did, because with his accident and then getting Motor Neurone Disease, it's not the average sort of bad luck is it? But I think that because of what happened to Mikie, hundreds of peoples' lives have been changed.

He spoke to so many people about God and many are now Christians as a result. He used to say that when he had Motor Neurone Disease that he was the happiest he'd ever been. Now I can understand that.

I've now got Mikie's Bible and I have all his notes inside it. I don't read it every day, but I read it a lot more than I did. I will pick it up and read it for 20 minutes at a time. Now a friend is introducing me to a church in Oxford. I've totally turned myself over into the hands of God to put me in whatever direction he wants to put me in. I am a very green horse. I'm not a polo pony yet. I've just come off the track and I've got two years before I can start to play polo. But I'm keen to learn.

David Heaton-Ellis now attends a church in Oxford, near his home in Headington. He writes, 'My faith has grown and is helping me greatly with every day life.'

4

'The pain wouldn't go away and I was just crying and crying. I said, "Lord, if this is it, just take me now." '

The story of Elisabetta Bell

One week after she accepted her boyfriend's proposal of marriage, Elisabetta Bell discovered she had cancer. For eight months she underwent agonising treatment. Here she tells the story and describes how God has been at her side throughout . . .

I grew up in a Christian family in Italy and we used to go to church, Sunday school and everything. When I grew older I was an exchange student in England for a while. Then I returned to England because I liked it so much and wanted to improve my English. I came back in 1991 and met my husband David at All Soul's, Langham Place. When he proposed to me we'd been going out for maybe five or six months. It was a lovely surprise. I was still in my twenties and I thought life was gorgeous and the future looked absolutely amazing. At the time he proposed, I felt I was going down with a bad cold and I was coughing quite a lot. But it was December and I just put it down to the English winter. I went back home to Italy for Christmas and explained to my family that this Englishman had proposed to me.

Then I came back to England. I felt that year was going to be such a wonderful year because my studies were going well (I was studying Music at the Royal Academy of Music) and David and I were soon to get married. But when I arrived back, the cold began getting quite bad. I had a bit of pain in my chest so I went to the local hospital – Homerton in east London – for them to give me some antibiotics perhaps. They did some blood tests and a chest X-ray and then said they wanted to keep me in to investigate a bit more. So they kept me in for a night and then the following morning they said they wanted to send me to Barts hospital in the City. I went in an ambulance and I was a little frightened. I wasn't expecting this at all. I didn't know why I was there. I just thought maybe I had a bad chest infection at that point. I didn't have a clue what it was.

Within a couple of days they gave me the diagnosis. The doctor came to my bedside and pulled the curtains round and said 'Well we think we know what it is. There are two options. It is either Leukaemia or Lymphoma.' I'd heard of Leukaemia and I knew that it wasn't good news. But I'd never heard the word Lymphoma before so I wasn't sure what it was. I thought maybe the bad news was the Leukaemia and the good news was the Lymphoma, so in my heart I thought, 'Oh dear, I hope it's the Lymphoma.'

They came back after a couple of hours and the doctor said, 'It's the Lymphoma'.

Then I asked, 'What does that mean?'

And the doctor sat down and said 'It's cancer.'

I asked 'Is it benign?'

And he said, 'No, it's highly malignant.' And then he explained that it was a tumour near my lungs. I was very surprised because up until two days before I had been leading a perfectly normal life.

They kept me in hospital for still more tests and as the days passed I had to be on oxygen because I was so bad. The doctors were amazed that I hadn't gone to hospital earlier because the cancer had spread so much in my chest. The tumour affected my lymphatic system and there was fluid all around my heart, which meant the heart was finding it hard to beat normally. There was also fluid from the lymphatic nodes into my stomach – so basically it had spread all over. I asked if I could go back home to Italy, but the doctors said there was no way because my lungs were too full of cancer. It wouldn't be wise for me to fly. I was a bit frightened but I felt God so strongly with me. I had gone throughout my life knowing God and knowing his love for me – but now I knew it even more powerfully. It was a bit like the Old Testament character Job, who said at the end of his sufferings, 'I knew you before but now I see you.' And that's the way I felt. At that time in hospital I knew God in a way I'd never known him before.

The day they gave me the news about the cancer, they said, 'We're going to have to give you chemotherapy' and they started straight away. There was no time to waste. I asked what chances I had and they said they couldn't say. They didn't know at that point if I would make it. I asked if the chemotherapy would get rid of the cancer and they said they didn't know that either. I didn't dare ask 'How long have I got?' I didn't want to know. David was the first person I told. He had already guessed that it was cancer because I was in the oncology unit. I didn't know that 'oncology' is where people go when they have cancer. I didn't have a clue but there were bald people around me, so I suppose I should have realised.

When I told David I said to him, 'Look, when you proposed to me I didn't know I had cancer and now I'm in this situation I don't even know if I'm going to be alive to marry you. You can go. You don't have to stick with me.' That was only fair wasn't it? But we both cried as I said it. Many people out there would freak out and run a mile if they heard the word 'cancer', but God was good to me because David had known someone close who had survived cancer. When he was young, his sister Sally had cancer of the bowel and had recovered. In answer to my question, David said words to the effect, 'I'm here and I'm here to stay.' I was very pleased!

The first thing the chemotherapy does is make you feel so sick. It's like poison. After the first lot of chemo it felt like fire blazing through my body. The chemo kills not just the cancer cells but all the good cells in your body so you are left with no immune system at all. You can catch a cold and die from it. You are very, very vulnerable to any infection. You also lose your hair completely. In addition, you lose so much weight that they have to give you steroids to build you up. So one moment you are very, very thin and the next moment you are all swollen up because of the steroids. You get the most horrendous mouth sores so they have to give you morphine to enable you to eat. Otherwise it would be just too painful. I had the treatment for eight months and was in Bart's Hospital for almost all that time. My mum was marvellous and came over to England to be with me for the whole time. It was great. She is a very strong Christian and has the most beautiful servant heart.

One night I was at home when I was suddenly in the most excruciating pain. They had to rush me in to hospital where the doctors simply did not know what was causing it. They thought that they would have to operate on me. I was in so much pain and they kept giving me more and more morphine but it wouldn't work. The pain wouldn't go and I was just crying and crying and I said, 'Lord, if this is it, just take me now because this is unbearable.' My mum was there and she just kept praying and praying. I could hear her voice, quietly, just praying and praying and she was in tears and I was in tears. But it was one of those moments when for some reason the pain stays there. It doesn't go (or the Lord chooses not to take away the pain immediately) but God is with you in the midst of the agony. My mum was an angel to me at that time because I couldn't formulate a prayer. I couldn't say anything. But she was there. She was praying on my behalf. We have always been very close but at that particular time I felt I didn't have to be strong or brave because my mum was there.

Of course I was engaged to be married through all this and you know if you are engaged you want to look at your best. And I remember thinking, 'I look awful. I've lost my hair.' Every time David came to the hospital I would think, 'I want to look nice for my fiancée' but then I would look in the mirror and I was absolutely disgusting! David has been a rock. He is such a strong, solid man of God. I remember very clearly coming out of one of the operations I had and they had to put a cannula tube in my chest because my veins had got so hard and the chemotherapy could not be administered through them.

As I came out of the theatre and was just coming around, David was next to my bed and he turned to me and said, 'You are so beautiful, I love you so much.' And there I was – such a mess. I didn't look beautiful at all. I was so bald at that point – I didn't have one hair on my head. I had lost so much weight. I didn't feel feminine in any way. And on top of all that I had this tube sticking out of my chest. But he was there saying, 'You are so beautiful. I love you so much. You are the most gorgeous woman I've ever met.' I really felt it was God himself speaking through David telling me, 'You are my precious darling. You are so beautiful to me.' I just remember that so clearly.

David used to come to the hospital and sit at my bedside and take my hand and say, 'Now darling, think that you are in Italy. The sun is shining; we are on the beach; we are going for a long walk. You can hear the waves pounding . . .' David has been my rock. Mum has been my angel. God really blessed me so much through both of them in those times.

In April 1992, in the middle of those eight months of treatment, I was at home feeling really poorly when a friend of mine came round and told me about a church meeting where they had a speaker called Jackie Pullinger.

She said, 'You must come to this meeting. This woman has got an amazing ministry. You must come.' So I got dressed and we went. I can't even remember which church it was. We got to this meeting and Jackie Pullinger was talking. For some time I had been feeling the Lord speaking to me through Psalm 126: 'When the Lord brought back the captives to Zion, we were like those who dreamed.' And I felt that the cancer was a bit like being in the desert. I wanted to get over it and go into a place of rest, but also for God to use this so that in the future I could help others going through the same thing. Another important verse for me was the one that says, 'Those that go out weeping will come back with songs of joy.' I don't think you fully understand that until you weep a lot.

When I started listening to Jackie, I realised she was talking about Psalm 126. She was basically encouraging people to move on in their walk of life from the 'time of desert' into a 'time of coming to the promised land.' As this was such an important passage for me, her words really spoke to me so deeply. At the end she asked people to come forward for ministry. And I went forward and people from her team came over. They asked what I would like prayer for and I explained about my illness. I asked if they could pray that God would turn around my situation so that I could be of help to others. They asked me, 'Do you want to be healed?' and strangely at that point I felt it didn't really matter. Yes of course I wanted to get over it and to lead a normal life, but that wasn't it.

I said, 'If God wants me to carry on without the cancer that's great, but my prayer is that somehow the situation will change so that I can help others.' That was more in my heart.

Eventually, Jackie came over and prayed as well. This was the first time that anyone had prayed for me by laying hands on me. I was wearing a wig and I remember they touched my wig and I started weeping because I felt so embarrassed. When you haven't got hair, it's odd but you feel almost naked in front of people. It's so humiliating. But the Lord was at work. I thought they were speaking in Chinese, but they were praying in tongues. Nobody had ever prayed over me in tongues. I left the meeting feeling absolutely exhausted but I felt really spiritually renewed inside. And I didn't have a clue at that point about what God was going to do, whether I'd survive or die. I really didn't know but it didn't matter. At that time we all thought I might die. I was in a hospital where I was surrounded by people fighting for life. And lots of them didn't make it. For me, I knew that even if I died I would be all right. That was a reality.

One night I thought, 'That's it. I'm going to die tonight.' I was in an isolation room and my mum had left and David had left and the only thing that I started fearing was that I was going to die by myself. I wanted to call Mum and David and ask them to come back to hospital and be with me because I was pretty sure I was going to die. I had a phone next to my bed and I turned round to reach for it but I was too weak. I really felt that life was draining away from me. I didn't have the energy to pick up the phone. So I thought, 'It's all right. I can just press the button for the nurse and she will phone home for me.' And I turned round to reach for the bell to call the nurse and I couldn't do that either. So I was in bed and all of a sudden, I thought, 'That's it, I'm dying tonight and I'll be by myself.'

I was so scared then for a fraction of a second. I really was scared. And then all of a sudden I felt the Spirit of God on me and I felt the Lord saying, 'You're not alone.' God was with me. I was safe. I didn't need anything else. I remember thinking, 'Lord, if you take me through this and I don't die, and I come out of this alive, and one day I lose my mum, my family, my friends, my house, my job, as long as I've got you, I know now I've got everything I need.'

So you see death is a real thing. When you go through times like this, you realise death is not something that may happen at some point in the future. It's something that you have to confront and fight every day. For me, it wasn't so much a fight, because I wasn't fighting at all: the Lord was doing it all for me one step at a time. One night in July of that year, I was in my room and I was at the end of my physical strength. The next day I was going to have a very important scan and

I prayed in my heart, 'Lord if they come back to me after the scan and say, "We need to give you more chemotherapy" I'm going to take it from you that that is the end and I'm going to say to them, "No that's it. I don't want any more." But if they come and say, "We want to give you radiotherapy" then I'll take it from you that you want me to continue and I'll go for it.'

With chemotherapy, you get injections through your veins and it makes you feel really sick. It takes weeks to get over it and makes your life absolutely dreadful. Your immune system is low so you are in isolation and you can catch anything and die from it. Radiotherapy is localised where the cancer is and you don't suffer from side-effects as much. You might just get burnt or whatever but you don't get sick, and your hair starts growing again, so that was good! Anyway, I tried to say this prayer but found I just couldn't. I know what I had in my heart and what I wanted to say, but I was crying so much that I couldn't say it. And then, I started speaking in tongues.

Nobody had ever prayed that I would speak in tongues to my knowledge. But this new language just came flooding through me and I was just talking. It was like a river of things just coming out and there were tears down my face and I knew I was reaching God's heart. I felt that God was reminding me through his spirit of the story of the woman who was haemorrhaging and she stretched out and touched Jesus' cloak. And as I lay on that bed, I just stretched out my hand because I so wanted to touch him. At that moment I knew that God was with me.

The following day I told my mum what happened. I

said, 'Mum, I was speaking in tongues last night' and I told her everything. I said to her 'Look, if they come back and say "More chemo" I'm going to say no and you'll take me home and I'll die. If they come back and they say "radiotherapy" then we'll take that as being from God and we'll go for it.' They took the scan and came back and they said 'radiotherapy.'

So I started radiotherapy and after that was finished they said, 'That's it, Elisabetta. We've given you all the treatment your body can stand. Now we have to see what happens.' I was left with this shadow on my chest (which still shows on X-rays to this day). It was smaller than the original shadow, but now it wasn't getting any smaller so they left it and they said, 'If it grows again then we'll have to give you some more treatment, but if it stays the same we'll just monitor it.'

That July, I went home and got better little by little and David and I got married at the end of July at All Souls. We really felt there was no time to waste because we felt I might die. Life becomes so precious. At the wedding, all the nurses from the hospital were there and it was a great celebration. When my turn came to say, 'In sickness and in health,' there was a silence and, apparently, all my nurses behind me were in floods of tears. But I was standing there just thinking, 'Lord, will you give me at least a year with David?' I still remember that. But it was a lovely, lovely special day. Life becomes so precious when you learn to live day by day. You don't think, 'Oh but what if in three years, or in a year, or in six months . . .'

They didn't tell me, but they were sure I would need to go back for more treatment. They said that if nothing showed up in the tests during the first two years after my treatment, the chance of the cancer returning would be 50/50. And nothing showed up. And I haven't had chemotherapy since. That was in 1992 and every year that goes by, it's slightly less likely, but still there's some chance. But it doesn't matter. It really doesn't matter. Whenever I go back to the hospital the consultant always calls in one of the medical students saying, 'Now let me tell you about Elisabetta,' because they really did not think I would make it. I was very bad. So still whenever I go there they think it's pretty amazing.

David and I have been married since 1992 and we are absolutely over the moon. We still think it's the first year. I think the shadow is still there to keep me on my toes. I've always been such a planner. Everything – my career, my job – was so carefully planned and I needed to learn to just give it up to God and learn how to lean on him and on his strength only. Although I thought I did I never really did it. I remember John Wimber talking at a conference some years ago after he had cancer and he said, 'I'm going to die the day that the Lord is calling me back home.'

And I thought, 'That's true. It's not the cancer. The cancer will never kill me. I'm going to go to heaven the day that the Lord wants me back home.' And with that in mind, really what can you fear? The Lord knows all the days of my life. He's planned them all. That's it, isn't it? It's wonderful!

Elisabetta Bell now attends St. Paul's Church, Hammersmith, with her husband David. She remains actively involved with chaplaincy work at the Royal Brompton

Hospital in London. One of the patients she prayed for at the Royal Brompton was Matthew Welch, whose story follows . . .

The story of Matthew Welch

Following a serious motorcycle accident, eighteen-year-old Matthew Welch was given 'hours to live' by doctors. He hung on to life, although his injuries were declared so great that he would remain a 'vegetable' for ever. This is the story of how his family and the hospital's chaplaincy team prayed – and how God answered. The story is told by his mother, Joan:

I originally come from up north and when I was young we used to go to Sunday school and church regularly. Then we moved down to Buckinghamshire when I was 10 and we rather stopped. Norman and I were married in 1973 and Matthew was born six years later. Our daughter Tara came along three and a half years after that.

Matt has always been interested in motorbikes. When he was 16, he got a moped and things graduated from there. He soon wanted something bigger. We were always quite against it as parents. We were naturally terrified of motorbikes because you haven't got the protection on bikes that you have in a car. But he had a real passion for bikes. He used to spend most of his time in the little motorbike shop around the corner in Taplow called 'Solo's'. He used to spend hours and hours there, building up bikes, helping them do all sorts of things.

Then he had a bike accident in August 1996 where he broke his left leg badly and we thought that was quite a catastrophe. A car pulled out in front of him and he flew over the handlebars. He was in hospital for two weeks and afterwards he swore he would never get on another bike and he didn't for a very long time. When he recovered he still spent a lot of his time round at Solo's.

Then, just after his eighteenth birthday in April 1997, he said he'd quite like to ride bikes again – but not on the road, just on tracks. He asked if we minded. We said, 'If we say no, you are going to do it anyway', so we said yes. He had already started to build up an old 250cc bike that Richard, the owner of Solo's, said he could have and he more or less virtually built it from the shell. Richard checked it to see that everything was okay and in September 1997 Matt started getting it ready for a track day. He brought the bike home on a Monday and I told him to be careful as he knew how I felt about him being on bikes.

He said, 'Yes, yes I know.' He tapped his leg and said, 'I know. It's painful.'

On the Wednesday evening, September 10, he and his father went for a pushbike ride down by the river along the towpaths. It was just after the death of Princess Diana and I was going out with my sister to Windsor Castle to place some flowers there for her. When I got home, I asked where Matt and Tara were and Norman said that Matt had gone out to 'put a few miles on that bike.' He also said that he'd had a phone call from Richard that Wycombe Hospital had been in touch to say that Quentin, this other guy who worked at the bike shop, had had an accident and he was asking if Matt could go up to the hospital to see how he was.

At about 10pm the phone went again and Norman answered it upstairs. When he came down he looked at me and he was grey.

He said to me 'Get your coat. It's Matt in hospital.' I thought, 'Oh God, no. Not again.'

The hospital had thought it was Quentin because the bike was still registered in his name. So Norman, Tara and I made our way to Wycombe General Hospital.

As soon as we got there, we were ushered straight away into a side room and in a couple of minutes a doctor and nurse came in. The doctor's white coat was covered in blood and he said 'I've got somebody here, but I'm not sure whether it's your son or not. He has lost so much blood and has so many injuries that we don't think he is going to make it.' I asked him if he had blond hair.

He said 'Blond hair? I'm afraid I've been too worried about saving his life to worry about the colour of his hair.'

I said that if it was our son, he's got a little dent in his left leg.

He said, 'Then I'm sorry. It is your son.'

I couldn't believe it was happening. We just waited in this other little room where a nurse made us tea. We all looked at the door handle waiting for news. It was unbearable. I didn't want to hear the news that he

David and Anne Kennedy
with Ralph and Alexandra

Ben Hume-Wright
with Anitra and Querida

Hélène
Murphy

David Heaton-Ellis

Judy Cahusac with Bill and George

Etam and Shabu Dedhar

David and
Elisabetta Bell

Pam and
Pete Sefton

Mike Norris

Hilary and David Medhurst

Ken Ashton

Mark and Carolanne Minashi with Alexander, William and Natasha

Jonathan Jeffes

Charles and Marijke Tapson with Daniel, Lydia and Benedict

Luther Blacklock and (inset) Janet Blacklock with Thomas

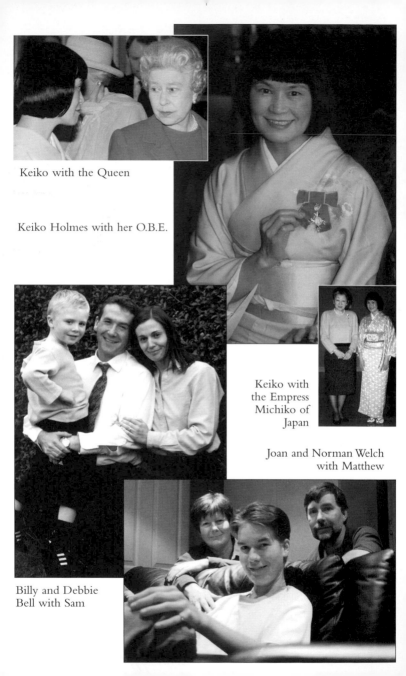

Keiko with the Queen

Keiko Holmes with her O.B.E.

Keiko with the Empress Michiko of Japan

Joan and Norman Welch with Matthew

Billy and Debbie Bell with Sam

hadn't made it. It seems as if he'd gone to Maidenhead and the police say that either he lost control of the bike or, possibly, that he heard a noise on the engine, stopped at the side and was tweaking the engine when something like a transit van came along and walloped him on the head and shoulder. Whatever it was, he was found in the bushes with the bike still running. There were no witnesses to what happened. He had been wearing his brand new blue and white leathers and a top-of-the range, really expensive crash helmet.

We were told Matt had lost almost the whole of one lung and he was being operated on. He had to have 28 pints of blood because he was bleeding internally the whole time. Finally, the doctor came and told us that they had him stable and he was in intensive care. I was desperate to see him but they were obviously still doing things to him. It was 3 or 4 o'clock in the morning when I was allowed to go in. Norman couldn't face it at the time. When I saw him his face was hardly recognisable. He was so swollen and had a great big gash on his chin. He had a fractured skull and two black eyes. He was on a ventilator and had a whole lot of tubes coming out of him.

The next day, the Thursday morning, my sister and her husband were with us and were sitting in the waiting room in intensive care. The doctor came in and said there was good news and bad news. The good news was that the head injuries weren't too bad. The bad news was that his lungs were in a really bad way. They didn't have the ventilators to support him at High Wycombe, so they had decided to rush him up to the Royal Brompton Hospital in Sydney Street, London.

They had wanted to use a helicopter, but because of the state of the lungs and pressure, they couldn't. They said he only had a 25 per cent chance of making the journey, but they had to give him that chance.

It took hours to set everything up, but the move happened that afternoon. Two doctors went with Matt in the ambulance and we followed on. When we got to the Brompton Hospital, we were taken straight to the waiting room in intensive care. Soon afterwards, one of the main doctors in intensive care, Cliff Morgan, told us that there was bad news. Norman and I looked at each other and thought 'What now?' Dr Morgan said that Matt's brain was still swelling and that his head injuries were quite bad after all. A courier had taken the scans of Matt's head round to the Chelsea and Westminster Hospital, where their top neuro-surgeon Nigel Mendosa was looking at them.

When it came, Nigel Mendosa's prognosis was not good. He said that Matthew had just hours to live. The brain was likely to continue to swell and our son would be brain dead. We asked what percentage there was of Matthew surviving and they said that with his serious lung injuries as well, his survival chances were not even one per cent. He had literally hours to live and wouldn't survive. It felt like a really bad dream. I went out to the waiting room. I was thinking 'Somebody pinch me! Wake me up! It was an absolutely horrendous time. I felt like a zombie as it seemed so unreal. My sister and some friends of Matt's from the motorbike shop were in the waiting room. Norman told them that Matthew had hours to live. There were lots of tears and my sister threw her arms around me.

We were allowed to see him, but when we walked in we could hardly recognise him. He had wires left, right and centre, and he had surgical emphysema which made him swell up like a Michelin man. He looked like if you stuck a pin in him he would pop. It was horrific. We had a couple of comfy chairs beside the bed and we just sat and held his hand.

One nurse called Vanessa kept asking my husband 'What can I do for you?'

He said there was only one thing, 'We need a miracle.'

The doctors couldn't understand how Matthew survived the night. The following day I asked if there was a chaplaincy. They asked what religion I was and I told them that I was Church of England.

Late on Friday evening, everything was looking really bad and they thought that Matthew's time had come. That was when the chaplain, Nicky Lee, came to see us. At that time, there was Norman, myself, my sister, brother-in-law and Tara – the real close family. We were standing around Matthew's bed and Nicky suggested that we hold hands while he prayed for Matthew and all of us. Nicky prayed a prayer in which he handed Matt over into God's hands and I remember thinking, 'Now it is up to God what happens.' It was hard to take it all in. I felt almost as if I'd died and I was looking down and could see this dreadful picture of us standing around my son's bed, the minister handing Matthew over to God.

Amazingly, Matt survived that night too. We saw a lot of Nicky after that. Matt continued to stay alive on the life support machine and the doctors kept looking into his eyes, but there was no sign of life. This went on for weeks and weeks. The doctors kept saying his pupils were 'blown' and that there was nothing there basically. We were told then that the left hand side of his brain – the side that controls all the movement on your right side and, in most cases, your intelligence and speech – was dead. Apart from almost having lost a lung, the other lung was bad as well. We were told that at best he was going to be a vegetable. I had that hammered into me day in, day out for six weeks and one day I just said to the doctors, 'Don't tell me, I don't want to know. I'm not stupid, I know he's critical, but when you have something new to tell me, please tell me. I can't take this any more.'

Throughout all this time, we were stroking his brow, holding his hand and playing his favourite CDs. They started reducing the sedation to see if he would do anything for himself. They were hoping to get some sign from the eyes – or some sign that he was trying to breathe for himself. But things looked bad and there came a time after about a month when they decided to test whether he was completely brain dead and they should switch the ventilator off. They even suggested we discuss whether to allow organ donations.

The tests were to be conducted by three consultants. The first did his tests and could find no signs of life at all. The second consultant then did three tests to see if there was any sign of life. Matt totally failed the first two, but on the third test there was a tiny flicker in one of his eyelids and that was enough for them to say that there was some sign of life. Some weeks later, a top neurologist came in and had a look at Matthew. He told us that he would be like a vegetable for the rest of his life.

I said, 'What about these cases where people have been in a coma for months and have come out of it?'

He said they were in the papers because they were 'one in a million' cases. So we really didn't get much joy from that.

Throughout all this time, David and Elisabetta [hospital chaplaincy team linked to Holy Trinity Brompton] used to come around and stand around the bed praying that he showed some sign of life, that his hand would move, that something would happen. They – and Nicky Lee too – would come round at least once or twice a week. I was spending a lot of time in the chapel, praying, asking for peace, help, anything!

Then came the tracheostomy. When patients are on a life support machine in intensive care for a long time, it can be very uncomfortable as the tube goes down through their mouth and they could lose their voice and suffer damage. So what they wanted to do was a tracheostomy where they put the tube directly through the neck. We were told by an Australian doctor that it was routine and wouldn't take very long. So on the Friday of week six we were told they were going to take Matthew down to the theatre to do this and we felt quite calm about it.

We were sitting in the waiting room with my nephew and his wife when the doctor came out in his theatre robe. He called us out and, with tears pouring down his face, he said, 'Something has gone wrong and we can't ventilate him. His blood pressure is so low that he is not going to make it. I'm afraid it is all my fault.

I'm going to lose your son.' Those were his exact words. After six weeks, you can imagine how we felt. The tears just flowed. I could not take this in any longer. Norman turned to Tara. She ran out and he followed her. Then, an hour later, the Australian doctor came back into the relatives' room where we all were, and said that he couldn't believe it, but everything had gone back to normal. The tube was back in Matthew's mouth and the life support machine was back on!

Throughout this time Matt was between one and two on the 'Glasgow coma scale', where healthy people who are alive and conscious are 15, and zero is dead. At this time, he was becoming resistant to most of the antibiotics and they kept saying to us that one of these days they were going to go to the cupboard and the cupboard would be bare.

My birthday was 30 October and I spent it at Matt's bedside talking to him about past birthdays and everything. People had been praying that something may happen that day, but there were still no signs of life from him. He was just lying there lifeless. That day the doctors told me they were going to have to try again with the tracheostomy. I was terrified and remember thinking, 'Oh my God, I don't want to go through that again.' But we were told there was no alternative and that it would be performed by the top consultant, Mr Goldstraw.

The following morning one of the doctors rang to say that the tracheostomy was going ahead but that there was a new piece of news. She (the doctor) had been in the room with Matt checking him over when she had taken hold of his hand and felt a slight squeeze.

We couldn't believe it. I was on the phone and such euphoria came over me that the tears were just streaming down my face. I said 'God, thank you.' I couldn't believe it. It really gave us so much hope that he was going to live. We got to the hospital at 2.30pm and went straight in to see Matt. I held his hand but I couldn't feel anything. He was just knocked out.

At quarter to four, Mr Goldstraw and his team just came into the room to perform the operation and we were then ushered to the waiting room. Afterwards, we were dying to see if it had been successful. Was the tube still in his mouth or was it coming out of his neck?

Norman just said 'Look, love, they've pulled the blinds up. The tube's coming out of his neck.'

It was wonderful to see his lips again, even though they were dry. He looked more like a person then than someone with just a machine stuck in him.

The next day, Saturday 1 November, we got to the hospital at 8.30am and heard the amazing news that Matt had opened one of his eyes very slightly. By the time we arrived, he was having problems with his ventilation. The doctors seemed to think this was because he was waking up more and getting anxious. It was wonderful news. We just wanted to run outside into Kings Road, London. It was just fantastic to have some real positive sign of life! But it all remained terribly slow.

A few weeks later, he began to open both eyes, though there was no recognition in them. You couldn't tell if he was looking at you or not. We kept thinking, 'Is this our Matt? How much brain damage is there and will he ever recognise us?' He did manage the occasional squeeze with his left hand, just slightly.

Then one day, nine weeks after the accident, I was sitting next to his bed on a stool holding his hand while the nurse was busy on the computer. All of a sudden his head moved and I shouted, 'Did you see that? Did you just see that? Matt, Matt! He moved!'

The nurse said, 'Oh, I don't think so.'

But I said 'I know he did, I know he did!'

I was watching his every move, his every breath! It was wonderful, fantastic, it really was!

Things went on from there until his head moved, then he opened both eyes. And then he did start to begin to understand what you were saying to him. We knew that because he would occasionally give a tiny nod when we were talking. Then he spoke his first words. Norman and I were just preparing to leave for home at nine o'clock one evening when he suddenly said quietly, 'Don't go Dad!' We leapt with excitement and rushed to his side. He said it again, 'Don't go.' I had tears streaming down my face. You see things like this on TV that are fictional, but this was real life.

But throughout all this there were troughs and peaks. The troughs were to do with the build-up of fluid in his lungs, the threat of meningitis at one time, and the fact that he started having fits. The peaks were when he started to move more and more. By the time Christmas came, he was moving his left hand slightly. On Christmas Eve the nurse said to us, 'Matt is going to have a nice surprise for you tomorrow morning.' The next day as we walked in, Matthew was lying there holding a large card in his hand. Inside, he had written

– with the nurse's help – 'To Mum and Dad and Tara, Happy Christmas, Love Matt.' It just broke my heart when I saw it. It was just so emotional. I cried and cried. He continued to progress slowly and become more and more aware of us all. It was a long time before he smiled, but even that happened eventually.

In early February, Angus Kennedy, the consultant neurologist who had been convinced Matt would be a vegetable, came to see him again. The doctors had liaised with him and they were all around the bed when he said to Matthew 'Say after me, Matthew: REPETITION.'

And Matthew said quietly 'Repetition.'

I couldn't believe it. It was fantastic. Mr Kennedy couldn't believe it either.

On 16 February, he was moved from the Brompton to High Wycombe Hospital. He had been in intensive care at the Brompton for 161 days – longer than anyone had ever done in the past. The nurses all got together to wave him off and they baked him a cake. It was quite a send-off.

He was in intensive care at Wycombe for a week and then they didn't know which ward to send him to. The problem was that he had a head injury, a lung injury, a crushed right shoulder which was inoperable, and a crushed arm which was so badly mangled, they couldn't do anything with it. They didn't know whether to put him in an orthopaedic ward, a respiratory ward for the lungs, or what. In the end they put him in an orthopaedic ward, where he stayed for another nine weeks. By this time he was off the life support machine, but he required oxygen 24 hours a day.

Then he was transferred from Wycombe to Amersham – which acted more like a rehabilitation centre – on his nineteenth birthday. He stayed there for another 12 weeks before coming home. While he was there, the doctors examined him and told us that he would never be able to walk because of the lung problem. He would just get terribly breathless. He came out of Amersham on 6 August, 1998 and we had a wonderful barbecue party with friends and family to celebrate. Matt was in a wheelchair in the garden and was talking quite fluently. The doctors never said it was a miracle, although the nurses did. Instead, the professor kept saying, 'He's an amazing kid.'

When he first came home, his bed was in the lounge because he couldn't get upstairs. He was very weak and vulnerable. We got a carer for him, but they and us literally had to do everything for him. By June 1999, he was writing with his left arm and his writing has improved from what it was before. His goal is that one day eventually he may be able to get a job and possibly work from home. Who knows? The sky's the limit after where he's come from!

Now he can walk across the room unaided, so that is another amazing step forward. He goes out occasionally and works on his computer and watches TV a lot. But he hates the epileptic fits he still gets occasionally. If you ask him, 'What is the worst thing about your injuries?' he would say it was the epilepsy. They have just increased his drugs and he's coping, although he doesn't like to be left alone. He could still do with a lung transplant. I have offered one of my lungs, but it's not that simple. In saying that, I look very positively on things and who knows?

This whole experience has strengthened my faith in God enormously. I have never prayed to God so much as I have done since this happened. I really feel that God has helped not just Matthew, but our entire family. He gave me the strength and carried me through the really harsh times when I really couldn't have coped alone. At times God was the only person who seemed to understand what I was going through. I can't stop thanking God for what he's done and I will always need him. One day in the Brompton on a Saturday in mid-December one doctor said to us in the waiting room when Matt was still not really showing great signs of life, 'I really do strongly believe in the power of prayer.'

David and Elisabetta prayed so often and there were so many joyous moments, so many times I thought 'God has played such a part in this.' I really needed the chaplaincy. It was a great source of comfort to me – and we had so many people, friends and relatives from different churches, praying for Matthew. I think it's absolutely wonderful and I continue praying daily. I continuously ask God to cradle Matt in his arms and give him his love and strength to help him get stronger all the time.

Elisabetta Bell, who helps lead the chaplaincy team at the Royal Brompton Hospital, describes here how she prayed for Matthew from soon after his arrival:

I remember Nicky [Nicky Lee, Chaplain of the Royal

Brompton Hospital] was called soon after Matthew arrived at the Brompton and it was thought he wouldn't make the night. After that, Nicky called me and I went and met the family. I had been in intensive care for the first time earlier that week when I had gone to pray for a ten-year-old boy called James who had a pacemaker and had collapsed at school. But he never regained consciousness and he died. I was devastated. I went home and cried to God, 'I can't do this. I can't pray for people and they die.' So when I started praying for Matthew, I just said, 'God, I'm not prepared to see another of our patients go like that.' When you pray for someone in a coma and their hand is warm, it really puts your faith to the test.

When I prayed for Matthew at the beginning, I confess that frankly I didn't have the faith – but I didn't show that to the family. I just said, 'Lord, we are begging you that this fellow will come back to life.' We just carried on praying at his bedside for quite a long time. I didn't know how to ask for a miracle. Early on, I asked one of the consultants, 'Can you tell me how he's doing?'

She said, 'Elisabetta, what you see is what you get. He will carry on as a vegetable. There is really nothing we can do.'

I never told Matthew's parents, but just thought, 'All the more reason to keep on praying.'

When I was in intensive care to pray with Matthew, I had to be covered in a plastic gown and wear gloves and a mask around my mouth. Just before the consultants came to see Matthew to decide whether or not to turn the life-support machine off, we prayed for a long time. I would sit gently next to him with my hand on his arm or sometimes on his head. I wondered if the nurses thought I was a nutter and I would always say, 'The family has given permission for me to pray.' But then, when one of the consultants found that glimmer of movement in one of Matthew's eyes, it was such an encouragement.

I just thought, 'YES! This is a sign from God to persevere, persevere . . .'

I used to visit him and pray with him at least twice a week. Often I would stay for an hour, although I would pray longer if Joan wasn't there. I used to pray, 'Lord, that he would hear your voice even now and know that you are with him.' When he came round and started to talk, he turned around one day and said, 'I love you.' I just wept. One day I sat next to him and said, 'I think the Lord has an amazing plan for you and that is why he has given you a second chance.'

Matthew has got such a great heart. I still feel the Lord will use him. He still needs lots of prayers. I thank God for Matthew that now I am not fearful about asking for miracles. When I go into intensive care now, I think, 'It happened before. It can happen again.'

Matthew Welch continues to live with his parents in Maidenhead. Joan Welch writes, 'It has been a very tough time for me both physically and mentally, but I continually thank God for Matt's life and the joy he brings me.'

5

'I prayed to God, "I know you don't believe in divorce but I don't love my husband any more. Can you change that?" '

The story of Etam and Shabu Dedhar

> *Etam and Shabu Dedhar, of Wellingborough in Northamptonshire, separated in 1994, after which their three children spent weekdays with one and weekends with the other. Divorce seemed inevitable. Then, at the end of 1996, Etam went on a local Alpha course which was the beginning of an emotional reconciliation...*

Etam's story

I had been brought up as a Christian attending the local Baptist church but it slipped away in my teens. When I married Shabu we had a big white wedding in a church because my parents wanted the best. I had a lovely dress and a car, top hat and tails – the lot – and Shabu went along with it. We married in 1983 and Shabu was working very hard as a chartered civil engineer and I was a trained chef. Then we had our three children very close together. Leigh is now 12, Nathalie, 11 and Oliver 10 and I was confined to the house looking after the family while Shabu was working very hard to support us. But I felt like a single parent as he took on more work to pay for a bigger mortgage on a bigger house. We communicated less and less and had some bad years. In July 1994 we split up. It was important to both of us that the children shouldn't suffer so we wanted to remain friends and work things out in a civilised way.

I looked after the children during the week and they stayed with their father at weekends. That was when I would go out with my girlfriends to pubs and clubs, smoking, coming back late. We each started – and ended – new relationships and were heading towards a divorce when a friend of mine asked me what I thought about religion. I said I'd always believed in God but usually more when things were going wrong. She invited me to church at the Wellingborough Christian Centre and said it would be a bit different. It certainly was. There was lots of clapping and dancing but I quite enjoyed it.

Then, in October 1996, she suggested I should try the Alpha course. I said yes out of politeness. I decided I would go once, say I hated it and then wouldn't go again. But I discovered I really enjoyed it and found it all so eye-opening. I realised I could have a relationship with God which I hadn't had before. I had always thought of Christians as rather weird people, but the people on Alpha were normal. I even met up with a friend who I'd been chatting to at a nightclub two days before. We said to each other, 'What are you doing here?' I loved the discussions but I wasn't too keen on the Holy Spirit day in the middle. Someone asked me if I would like them to pray for me and I said no thank you. That wasn't my kind of thing. But then a strange thing happened after I had been to the talk about healing. I just couldn't accept it and I asked God to give me some kind of proof.

Not long afterwards I was speaking to Shabu about the children and he was in real pain with his neck. He could hardly move his head so I offered to go and give him a massage. When I got there I asked if I could pray for him and I put my hands on his neck and he felt this warmth. A few hours later his pain had gone. I could hardly believe it. I started going to church more regularly.

By the end of the course I felt completely different and I went to talk to the pastor and said I felt as though I was standing on the edge of a cliff. I thought I was being asked to jump over the precipice proclaiming I was a Christian as I went down, but I didn't know where I was going to fall. I was just totally scared. He said he thought I already had jumped and that God was there in everything I did. Then I realised I had jumped and become a Christian. By the end of that year I could definitely say I had changed.

God helped me give up smoking in an extraordinary way. I didn't want to give up but one day at work I rang a friend and I could hear her smoking down the phone and I said: 'Oh don't do that. I haven't had a cigarette all day and you're making me long for one.' She said that she couldn't work all day without a cigarette and I felt that what she said was a message from God telling me, 'You can go all day without a cigarette.' That evening I was going to see a friend who doesn't smoke so I grabbed my cigarettes and thought I would wait until we'd eaten and then slip outside for a quick one. She was moaning about me smoking but when I went off for a smoke I found the cigarettes weren't in my bag after all. I had left them at home. I stayed with my friend overnight and went straight to the office the next day and did another day without smoking. And that was it. I realised I didn't need to smoke and I haven't had a cigarette since. I changed over the months and I started staying in with a takeaway instead of going out to clubs at weekends.

At first I felt I had given up my nightclubs but I couldn't see what God had given me in return. Somehow I knew he wouldn't just let me sit there and that I would be OK. Gradually I started thinking about my marriage. Shabu and I saw each other for the sake of the children on family occasions and we used to joke about being like a happy family. We went together to see a school for Leigh and realised we had to give separate addresses and that seemed strange. Eventually I prayed to God and said: 'I know you don't believe in divorce but I don't love my husband any more. Can you change that?' At the same time, some friends at church began to pray that we would get back together again.

Not long afterwards Shabu and I had to communicate a lot by mobile phone and we used to do it with text messages as it was cheaper than speaking. I found I began to miss it when he hadn't sent me a message. I began to feel a bit like you do when you're waiting for a love letter. And our relationship improved.

We were having a family dinner one Sunday in December 1997 and Shabu began asking a lot of questions about the church. So I invited him to come along and I was so surprised when he said he would. When we all walked in together as a family I could hardly believe what was happening. He continued to come to church each Sunday and within four weeks we decided to get back together. On the day we told our children the news, we all sat around the kitchen table. As we told them, Oliver looked up at the ceiling. It seemed as if he was trying to keep his tears in.

I said, 'What are you doing?'

He said, 'It's the best day of my life.'

After that, we were all crying. It was just unbelievable. We have gone to church as a family ever since – and things are so different now. Both Shabu and I have been baptised and so have two of our children.

Shabu and I pray together now – and with the children too. We are so secure in everything we do because we know our marriage is for life. Jesus is just everything to me. He is my friend and I couldn't do anything without him. I know he's there guiding me every day. I am sure that if I hadn't gone on Alpha, we wouldn't be back together. It is like a fairy tale.

'Our lives have changed dramatically.'

Shabu's story

I was excused Religious Instruction at school and was brought up without any religious education at all. I don't remember my parents expressing any particular beliefs, but I have always been open minded about religion. I was happy to be married in a church but it was really just to please Etam and her parents. When our children were born I was working long hours to earn the money for a bigger mortgage as we needed a bigger house. It was difficult and in those years we drifted apart. I noticed a change in Etam when she started going to church. She stopped going out with some of the people she knew who were a bit wild. We had been through some bad times and we had both had other relationships. But I felt Etam and I had established a stability for the children even though we were apart.

Sometime at the end of 1996, I suffered a sprain in my neck. It had been getting progressively worse over three or four days and although I had seen an osteopath, nothing seemed to work. The pain was very bad indeed. Etam offered to come and give me a massage and, while she was with me, she asked if she could pray for me. Then she started to massage my neck again and

I experienced this sense of warmth and heat. About two hours later the pain had gone and my neck felt completely better. I was a complete sceptic, but acknowledged that my recovery followed Etam's prayers.

When Etam asked me to go to church I thought I'd go and see what it was like. I'd never really been comfortable in a church but I found the experience in Wellingborough Christian Centre was completely different from what I expected. There was a lot of clapping and singing and I enjoyed it. Once I started going to the church I didn't stop. We would go together every Sunday. A lot of things in my life seemed to come into perspective when I was in church. I began to see how God may have been at work at different times in my life.

Etam and I discussed getting back together some weeks later but I had doubts about risking it because of the bad times we had had before. Yet it seemed God told us to take all that bad stuff and throw it overboard. It was as though God had taken the whole weight of what had gone wrong and said 'I've forgiven you.'

In January 1998, our church presented the drama 'Heaven's Gate and Hell's Flames'. It was a very simple story and very moving. At the end, someone stood up and asked everyone to shut their eyes. Then he said, 'If you would like to give your life to Jesus, slide your hand up.'

Then he asked everyone who had put their hands up to come forward. When I stood up to go forward, I found my son Leigh walking beside me. It was quite emotional and felt very important for the togetherness of our family.

Our lives have changed dramatically. I am a Christian in heart and mind and that affects what I do at home and at work. I think my attitude to people has changed and I look more closely at how I live my life. Our whole lifestyle has changed. We normally go to church twice on Sundays and I go to a men's group at 6am on Tuesday mornings. We have a very strong youth group in our church that our children attend. I am so grateful for this influence in their lives. As for our marriage, it is as if all the bad stuff has been taken and thrown out. I now have a realisation that Jesus took all my sins on the cross. We do not have to dwell on any past sins or analyse fault. We have been given a completely clean sheet. I can't think of any marriage guidance course that can do that.

Shabu and Etam Dedhar remain closely involved with their local church, where they run a house group. In September 2000, they celebrated their sixteenth wedding anniversary by renewing their marriage vows in a special ceremony at the church.

'You get people on telly who say, "My husband is my best friend." Well, Pete was never my best friend and I was never his. But he's my best friend now.'

The story of Pam and Pete Sefton

> *For 18 years, Pam Sefton hardly ever saw her husband Pete smile. Then she was invited to attend an Alpha course and later persuaded Pete to do the same. Here they describe what happened:*

Pam's story

I don't ever remember going to church as a child. It was only when I married my first husband who was a Catholic, in 1969, that I started going to Mass on a Sunday with him. I liked it straight away and we had two children, Laura and John, who were brought up in the Catholic faith. But I should say church was just a routine to us and no one ever mentioned the possibility of having Jesus in your life. We continued going to church regularly until our marriage broke up in 1976. We divorced two years later. Immediately after my marriage break-up, it was my friends in the church –

St George's, Eastfield, near Scarborough – who kept me going really. I think if I'd had nobody then it would have been really hard.

In early 1979, I was working in a local supermarket and the milkman who delivered milk there was a fellow called Pete. We met and got married in September 1979. For two years, I went to church with the children on my own, but then I invited Pete on a 'Marriage Encounter' weekend and he really enjoyed it. After that, he came to Mass on Sunday with me. Some time afterwards, Pete was made redundant and we moved south to Camberley in Surrey, where my sister lived. The move seemed so right because the house we lived at in Scarborough was number 71 and our new house was number 17. Also, both were painted red and white, so we just thought, 'Oh we're meant to be here.'

Pete got a job as a security guard and we started going to a local Catholic church. When you've lived up north and you come down to London, you find people are very different. We got quite disheartened with the church and didn't make friends. We just didn't seem to get anything from it. We used to come home and say, 'I don't know why we bother going. God never listens to us. He never answers our prayers.' It just got worse and worse and in the end we just said, 'We're not going to bother going any more.'

About a year after we stopped going to church, I went to work for a lady called Annie Walden, who was a member of a church called the Beacon Church in Camberley. She ran a Bed and Breakfast and I used to help her clean in the mornings. I used to be quite envious of her because she was always talking about

God all the time. I used to think to myself, 'I'd love to feel about God like that.' To see somebody so enthused about God, I used to think, 'I don't know where I've been.'

Every now and again I would pick my Bible up and try to read it. One night, I was reading and I said to Pete, 'I'm going to ring Annie Walden to tell me where to start reading the Bible.' When I phoned her, she said, 'Why don't you come to the Beacon with me on Sunday? We have a lovely pastor and you'll love it.'

I said, 'I'll see.'

I said to Pete, 'I might try the Beacon on Sunday.'

He said, 'What do you want to go there for? We're Catholics.'

And I said, 'But we don't go to church.'

'Well, you don't want to go down there,' he said.

So, I said, 'Well, I'm going to go anyway, because she's asked me.'

So I went on the Sunday and I didn't want to leave, but I had our daughter Laura coming for dinner at 12, so I had to walk out as the service was finishing. When I got home, I told Pete, 'It's great. I'm going to go back next Sunday.'

But again he said, 'What do you want to go there for?'

So I said, 'Well, you go down to the Catholic church then. I'll go to the Beacon.'

'I don't want to go to church,' he said.

Soon afterwards, Annie said to me, 'They're starting an Alpha course here in a couple of weeks. You ought to put your name down for it. They say it's really good.' I thought, 'I'll try anything.' So I put my name down for it. I asked Pete if he would come with me but he said, 'No, I won't. I don't need to find out about God.' I started Alpha in summer 1997 and I was hooked straight away. There were 10 or 15 people in the church hall and we watched the video. I just thought, 'This is for me.'

I had never thought about Jesus before. I knew Jesus was God's Son and he came down to earth and he died for our sins but that was about it really. I just thought that a Christian was someone who went to church on a Sunday, came home, tried to be good and then went back the following Sunday.

As Alpha went on, I used to come home and want to tell Pete everything. After I came in, I used to think, 'He'll ask me in a minute' but he used to just sit there reading the paper and watching the telly. Finally, I'd say, 'I had a really good night tonight.' 'Did you?' he'd say. And that would be the end of it. By the time of the weekend, I couldn't get enough. I was just so excited about God. I was prayed for and I had this feeling like an electric shock going right through my body. I just sat on my little bed there and I couldn't stop crying. It was just so emotional. I was so excited that Jesus was in my life. My only frustration was the thought that I'd been going to church all those years and I'd missed all this. I could have known about Jesus 30 years ago if I'd been told about him.

I invited the Beacon's pastor, Mark Landreth-Smith, round to our house a couple of times, but whenever he came, Pete would leave the room and go into the kitchen. He was very, very unsociable and abrupt with people – quite rude really. At the end of the course, we had the Alpha supper and I asked Pete to come. He said, 'No I won't. They sound an odd lot to me. I'm not going there.' I said, 'But if you don't go, you won't know. Just come and meet them and see that they are normal people.'

So finally he agreed to come – and he quite enjoyed it. After that I managed to persuade him to come to a Sunday service at church, but he felt a bit uncomfortable because it was so informal after what he had been used to. So I said, 'Why not come to the first night of Alpha and see if you like it? If you don't like it, you don't have to keep going.' So he agreed – and my best friend, Amanda Best, who wasn't a churchgoer either, also agreed to come on the course.

In the end, Pete completed the whole course and even agreed to help at the next one. It was at a training session for that second one that he invited Jesus into his life – and he has been a different man ever since. He just changed overnight. He just changed dramatically. He had always been so aggressive all the time but now he wasn't.

Before we both became Christians, we were married but we were like two single people being married. He went to work and did whatever he wanted to do – and I went to work and did my own thing. We didn't see much of each other and I resented that. But when God came into our lives, he gave us a marriage. You get people on telly who say, 'My husband is my best friend' – well, Pete was never my best friend and I was never his. But he's my best friend now. I've had a photo of Pete laughing enlarged and put up in the living room because that's what God has given me. He's given me that lovely smile on his face that I never had for about 18 years. Our son came in one day after Pete had been on the Alpha course and said to him, 'Who are you?' Then he asked me, 'What have you done with my Dad?' Everyone has seen a change in him.

We used to go on holiday and we never talked to anybody. We always sat on our own because Pete would never mix. It's like there's been a man inside him that's been trying to get out all these years and God's just opened the door and let this man out – and he's a lovely, lovely man. We're all getting the benefits now.

He's just been on a men's weekend with the church and he's been climbing up walls and walking on wires and playing water polo and stuff. I would never have imagined him doing anything like that. Now, when we go to church on a Sunday, he's off and he's mixing with everybody. They all think he's lovely and people say to me, 'Isn't your husband funny? He's always smiling,' and I sort of think to myself, 'Well, he wasn't always like that.' I know we all change, but you don't change from what Pete was like to what he is now – not without God. We do still have problems, but now we give it all to God and, whether things turn out good or bad, we accept that God has a plan for us.

I've learnt now that when you pray, it doesn't necessarily happen the day after or the minute after. Some things do, but some things you have to wait for. It's all in God's time. Our house is just full of God now. I know it is. I just wish that you could put a video in the video machine which would give you the feeling of what you feel when you've done an Alpha course. You wouldn't have to advertise. I've been on six Alpha courses and I love to see people change like they do. I could do an Alpha course all the time. I just love it.

'I used to go to the kitchen or out into the garden to hide.'

Pete's story

When Pam started going to Alpha, she would come back all excited and I thought she was different. She seemed more relaxed. She wasn't tense like she used to be at times. But I began to feel like I didn't have a wife any more. When Mark, the church pastor, or Hilary, the co-ordinator of the Alpha course, came to visit Pam, I used to go to the kitchen or out into the garden to hide. I was a bit shy. I used to say about Hilary, 'She's not getting hold of me.' Finally, after a while, Pam asked me to the Alpha dinner and I said, 'Yeah, I might as well. I'll just see what it is like.' So I went and I was surprised how normal the people were. They were quite friendly. In fact I began to enjoy it and when I had to miss an evening because of my shift work, I would think, 'Oh dear, I'm missing Alpha again tonight. I hope I can catch up.'

I finished the course and said I would help on the next one. At one of the training sessions for that, we all prayed for each other and I just said, 'Please God, come into my life.' I knew I had been fighting against inviting him in, but I couldn't fight it any more. As I said the prayer, I felt my legs go all weak. After that, I knew that he was with me 24 hours a day and he was always there. I started praying to him when I was at work and I noticed myself changing because when I swore, I would say, 'Sorry Lord.' Now my life has changed so much. I know Jesus is with me all the time and that he loves me.

One Sunday, our pastor Mark was praying for 'lost sons'. I was married before and have two sons, Philip and Gary, who I had not seen for 23 years. When Mark said this, I prayed that they would get in touch sometime. On the following Wednesday, Pam rang me up at work and said, 'Pete, I hope you're sitting down. I have to tell you something.'

She said, 'I've got a letter from Philip.'

I said, 'Philip who?'

She said, 'Your son.'

I was shocked. It was the answer to my prayer. The letter started, 'Dear Dad' and spoke of how he wanted to get in touch. It ended, 'Your loving son, Phil.' I wrote back to him straight away and we've been corresponding ever since. I haven't met him yet – he doesn't feel quite ready yet – but we have sent photographs and he has sent us photographs of his family. I've told him that I have become a Christian and said, 'You'll see a change in me.'

Pete and Pam Sefton continue to attend the Beacon Church near their home in Camberley. Pete says, 'God has given me a new life.' Pam says, 'God has put such a happy feeling in my heart. Life with Pete just gets better and better. What a wonderful God.'

6

'Sundays were our special time for
gardening and going out with the dogs.'

The story of David and Hilary Medhurst

> *David and Hilary Medhurst were happy with their
> lifestyle and didn't want to change it. They were
> invited on their local Alpha course and decided to
> go ahead because it would give them 'ammunition'
> for future debates with Christians. After the first
> night of Alpha, they sat in their kitchen and shook
> hands on a strange agreement: they would NOT
> become Christians. Here, Hilary tells their story . . .*

I was brought up in Northern Ireland, where my
family regularly attended a church which was very
strict. As I grew up I wanted to become less and less
involved. In 1975 I left Belfast to go to England to

teach, and got married in 1978. At that time we attended church regularly. During the summer of 1982, my husband left me. I was totally devastated and it was a very trying time for the whole family. Divorce was unheard of amongst Christians in Northern Ireland, but my family were fantastic and gave me a huge amount of support. Nevertheless, I lost all of my confidence and felt terrifically ashamed. I felt that I needed a real break, so I made a conscious decision to change as many things in my life as I could. I stopped going to church completely, and a short while afterwards met David through some close friends. I was still terribly hurt and after seeing him a couple of times I told him to just go away and leave me alone. Fortunately he kept in touch – and we eventually married in 1985.

David and his family were very cynical about Christians and anything to do with the church and that suited me just fine. After my previous experiences I was only too happy with the new format of Sundays. We built a lovely life for ourselves, and Sundays were our special time for gardening and going out with the dogs. Life was pretty good – a bit tight financially, but pretty good all the same. About this time there was another change in the family. My sister, Wilma, left the church in Belfast which our family had always attended and began to attend another. I was amazed at the difference in her. She had a very real faith and I was delighted for her – but I didn't want to discuss it. It all seemed so irrelevant to me. David was involved in doing a lot of charity work and we spent a lot of time organising balloon races and things like that. We certainly didn't need any involvement in anything else.

The only time we went to church was when we went home to Belfast. David really enjoyed going to the church attended by my sister and her husband, the Christian Fellowship Church, because sometimes a wonderful singer called Marie Lacey would sing and he loved listening to her.

In May 1997 the Christian Fellowship Church was ten years old and Marie Lacey was asked to write and direct a celebration to be held in the new Waterfront Hall in Belfast, which had been opened by Prince Charles and Kiri te Kanawe shortly before. My sister and her husband invited us as they were in the choir and we decided we would go, mainly because they were so excited about it, but also because it would be an opportunity to see my parents as well.

I went over two days earlier than David and went to one of the rehearsals. The production was called 'Victory' and I just wasn't prepared for what I saw. The style of the music was very black gospel, which I love, but there was also dance, drama and some superb audio visuals. It began with Creation and went through the Death and Resurrection of Jesus Christ, to the Second Coming. Sitting through the rehearsal, I was struck by the fact that everyone around me was working as a team. The people making the tea were every bit as important as the soloists and dancers, and the people painting the scenery were valued as much as the musicians. A lot of effort had obviously been put into this, and I looked forward to the performance. It was fabulous. A large number of people had come from Dublin to see it. The programme blurb stated: The divisions in the church not only mirror those in society, but perpetuate them. We want to play our part in being a healing agent, not only to Ireland but to the nations. We liked that.

I felt very unsettled after Victory, but couldn't put my finger on the reason. David did too, and although we both agreed that we had been really impressed by Victory and the people we'd met, we didn't really do anything about it.

On their next visit to England, Wilma and Ron introduced us to a couple called Liz and Dudley Sloggett who live near us and are Christians. We had such a good time in their company, and discovered that they were involved in an Alpha course in their church, Holy Trinity Claygate. We were invited to attend and after much discussion we agreed to give it a try. To be honest I was amazed that David ever expressed interest, but he said he knew very little about what being a Christian meant and felt that if he did this course he might learn enough to fend them off – my family in particular. I agreed to go along too – only because we do most things together.

The course was a small one – about eight people plus the Vicar and his henchmen. I felt hemmed in, trapped. After the talk we had a good discussion and David asked a lot of questions along with another person who had similar reservations. I didn't say anything at all – but it was interesting. Just listening to what was said made me realise that there was a great deal I had never understood. Listening to what was said in 'plain English' explained a lot.

In the car afterwards we agreed it had been more interesting than we'd expected. OK, so a lot of it made sense. Yes, it was good to have some answers, but there were bits that I hadn't liked. It came as a bit of a shock to hear that we did not measure up to God's perfect standards. We thought of ourselves as decent people – look at the charity work we'd done. We would always help friends in trouble and are kind to children and animals. I got home feeling depressed.

We sat down in our kitchen with a glass of wine and decided to set some ground rules. This Alpha thing was all right, but it must not be allowed to get out of hand. So we decided:-

1. Neither of us would become a Christian.
2. All invitations by the Vicar (or others who looked remotely as if they might be Christians) would be politely but firmly refused.
3. At absolutely no time would we agree to take part in any church activities, even those masquerading innocently as rambles or picnics.
4. Sundays would remain for the purposes of gardening, walking our two Westies, William and Henry, reading the papers and snoozing.

We shook hands on the deal and toasted the future by clinking glasses. Frankly I felt a lot safer after that.

As the weeks went on, however, I found that I was listening a lot more, especially when we had videos and Nicky Gumbel was speaking. David continued to ask questions. He wanted proof – proof of the actual existence of Jesus Christ and so on. Someone suggested he read a book called *Who Moved the Stone?* by Frank Morison. It was written by a barrister who had set out to disprove the gospel accounts, but who ended up being convinced by them. It was right up David's street. A few nights later I realised he had swapped his John Grisham for a Frank Morison. In fact he kept waking me up to read bits to me.

In November 1997 David needed to go to Belfast on business, so we decided to take a few extra days there. He had approached his company about taking early retirement, and we'd more or less decided that if they agreed we'd move over there. The plan was that we'd make a huge amount of money selling our house in Surrey, and buy a palace for a fraction of the price in Northern Ireland! It also meant missing an Alpha evening which I felt would be a welcome break. When we walked into my sister's home in Belfast, the first thing she said was, 'I hope you don't mind, but it's our Alpha meeting tonight. I asked the group if they'd mind if you joined in and they said of course not.' I was absolutely livid, but cheered up when I realised there were some as sceptical as me! It was quite good really and I ended up enjoying myself thoroughly putting lots of cats amongst lots of pigeons.

On the Sunday morning, we went to church because David wanted to hear Marie sing. I just sat and thought about what would happen to us. Where would we live? What would it be like? I have never felt so miserable in all my life. Then, when Paul Reid began to speak, I felt as if he was speaking to me. As I sat there, I suddenly realised that what I really needed to do was to give my life back to God. As the service ended, my sister saw that I was in a bit of a state and asked what the matter was. I said I wanted to give my life back to

God, but couldn't and explained about my promise to David. David put his arms around me and said it didn't matter. 'Go ahead,' he said. 'I don't mind.'

Wilma and Marie prayed with me and I asked God to forgive me for the things I'd done wrong. I felt terrible about breaking my agreement with David. I asked him if he wanted to become a Christian too but he said, 'No, not at the moment.' I was disappointed, but also very worried. I couldn't see myself going to church on my own – it just wouldn't work – and anyway I didn't want any barriers at all between us. Being a lone Christian would be a pretty tall order, and I didn't think I would be up to it. When we got back home I started to pray. I'd wait until David had gone in the mornings. One morning, I said, 'Look God, it's like this. David and I are a team. Help me through this. Show me what to do and say – because I haven't got a clue.'

The following Saturday we went into town and on our way back to the car passed one of the big music stores. There was a display of Barbra Streisand's new album *Higher Ground* by the door, so we bought a copy as a friend had told us how good it was. We were tired when we got back and we settled down with the Chinese Takeaway menu, a glass of wine and the new album. I was a bit gloomy, because the following morning I'd have to be very strong indeed if I was to leave David and go to church. I really didn't relish the thought at all – I'd be breaking yet another agreement! After listening to a few tracks, the song *Holy Ground* came on. It was phenomenal. I looked up at David and was surprised to see tears streaming down his face.

'What's the matter?' I asked him.

'It's the music' he said. 'I just can't get all this stuff out of my mind.'

'What stuff? You mean about becoming a Christian? Well, why don't you then? Just do it! Put us all out of our misery!'

'Well, I'm getting very close,' he said.

'Look, why don't you just put up or shut up?' I said. I couldn't believe I'd said such a stupid thing, but it just came out of my mouth.

'All right' he said.

I just stared at him. It wasn't at all the answer I was expecting. We needed a vicar, or someone else who knew what to do, but there was only me! So I took a deep breath and said 'Right, let's pray!'

We sat down and prayed a very similar prayer to the one that I'd prayed only six days before and David accepted Christ into his life.

Afterwards he said 'I'd expected it to be a huge leap . . . you know like in Butch Cassidy and the Sundance Kid, when Paul Newman and Robert Redford were on the ledge overlooking a deep gorge. They'd shot off all their bullets and the only place to go was down . . . into the river. In fact it was just a step! When you become a Christian you just step across the chasm, and then when you're over, you look back and wonder what all the fuss was about!'

The next day we went to church together, as Christians. God had really answered my prayer – I hadn't had to face even one Sunday going to church without David. It was very exciting – a new and very different phase of our lives had begun, and has continued.

Recently, David had to leave very early to drive to Manchester and rang me on his car phone from somewhere on the motorway. He said he'd really missed praying together before he left and suggested that we pray then. It shows how we've changed.

We're constantly being asked how becoming Christians has changed us, but I've now decided that it's much easier to say which aspects of our lives have remained unchanged – but I really can't think of any! We thought our life together was pretty good before, but we've just watched it get better and better. At the moment we still don't know where we'll end up living, but we do know that God will show us where, and that it will be just right for us. Before, the future was the great unknown, a sort of black hole full of worries and frantic calculations. Now, we just look forward to it!

David and Hilary Medhurst moved to Northern Ireland in December 1998, where they are now members of the Christian Fellowship Church which played such a part in their story.

'I didn't even eat the food for the first few weeks because I thought it might be drugged.'

The story of Mike Norris

When Mike Norris attended the Alpha course at Holy Trinity Brompton, he was so suspicious of everything that he feared the food might have been drugged. He refused to eat or drink anything for the first few weeks. Here he describes how his attitude changed . . .

My parents were divorced when I was quite young and I was brought up by my mother. I have got three sisters and two half sisters on my father's side. I went away to boarding school when I was 11 years old. I got confirmed when I was 13 because two of my friends had been confirmed and one had been given a nice bike and the other had got a snazzy watch. So I was a bit gutted when my mum presented me with a symbolic beeswax candle for my efforts. I never had any doubt that God existed but not Jesus Christ. I suppose I thought Jesus was just a fairy tale – a man with watery eyes who was quite kind and good to have on a picnic if you didn't have much food.

I got into a bit of trouble at school with smoking, drinking, and women (all fairly ordinary behaviour for someone at that age). One thing that did happen at school which was quite significant was a visit from the London Community Gospel Choir, who came to sing in the chapel one evening. I was about 17 and my mates and I all went along with a view to having a laugh at their expense. I thought it was going to be very boring but when we turned up there was an amazing atmosphere. They started singing some songs and the roof came down. One of the girls got up and started to dance with my history teacher in the aisle and then the whole school started dancing in the aisles and standing on the pews. Everyone was caught up in it – the sense of freedom – but it was respectful too. It was extraordinary that the school let that happen and it had a great impact. It was a fantastic thing.

When it was over, a friend invited me to join a group of them for a cigarette and I said no, which was quite unusual for me. I just wanted to go off and have a cigarette on my own and think about what had happened. I was really struck by something that night. It was God but I didn't necessarily make that link. I just thought, 'Wow, that was amazing. There was something going on there.'

When I left school, I took a year out and lived on a kibbutz in Israel for three months. We were based in northern Israel, living in little shed-type dormitories. It was completely unreligiously-motivated. A couple of mates were going there because they had heard that it was a cheap, boozy holiday – so I hooked up with them. In the end we arrived to find it was just us and a few other blokes and about 40 Scandinavian and English women. We couldn't believe our luck when we got there. I worked out in the fields with a team of about eight Hebrew men and used to sit on the back of a funny tractor and stake irrigation lines. Some of the people on the kibbutz had been in concentration camps and had numbers tattooed on their arms. It was a reality check – a time of growing up. I was very struck by Israel and enjoyed visiting the sites where Jesus was meant to have been born, lived and died. I was moved to sit in the Church of the Holy Sepulchre, the site of the tomb of Jesus and felt quite in awe, but I was still a long way off.

Just after I returned from the kibbutz, my father died very suddenly when he was still fairly young. I turned completely against God through the pain of it. I became very angry, saying, 'If God's good, why has my father died?' I became very anti-God. I never thought God wasn't true. I just thought, 'I want nothing to do with you.' It was a terribly painful time. Shortly afterwards I started at Reading University. I entered into life there and met some great people but kept my sadness under wraps. I worked hard (I studied law) and played hard – doing lots of sport and socialising.

In 1991, I went to law school in Guildford and on the first or second day I saw this amazing woman. She seemed to have something about her which was very attractive, but I couldn't quite put my finger on what it was. I didn't speak to her but I thought, 'I'd like to get to know her.' So every time I saw her I used to ask her what the time was and where the canteen was and in the end we became friends. It turned out that she was a Christian and I ended up going out with her. She sincerely believed the Bible but on that I just thought, 'How sweet, but you're very damaged!'

We had been going out for a few months when I went to her church for the first time. There were about 150 people on a Sunday morning and she was pleased I was going with her. I felt the nudges going round the church from her friends, 'This is her boyfriend who isn't a Christian.' It was awful. For a start, they didn't meet in a church, but in a school hall and I thought, 'Where's the spire?'

When someone read from the Bible, they all followed it in their own Bibles, taking notes, and I just thought, 'You are very, very odd.' I was quite frightened by it all and I thought I needed to help this girl who was clearly too deep in the wrong pool. Then they started singing some mindless gibberish together and I didn't know what it was. I just thought, 'Enough's enough, I am getting out of here.' But I was in the middle of a row and everyone had their arms out and their eyes shut so I couldn't get past them. I was panicking. Then I noticed there was a fire exit and I thought, I am going to have to set fire to the building if I'm going to get out. So I got my lighter out to set fire to my chair. Luckily all the gibberish suddenly died down. But I was just out of it by then. It was absolutely awful

I respected my girlfriend, but she was beyond saving from all this business. She was a rampant Christian and used to talk about Jesus on buses and trains. She used to invite me around to dinner and there would be about 15 Christians and me. They would all look at me as if I was meat. They were determined to convert me. I used to time how long it would be before they changed the subject to Jesus with monotonous predictability.

All this time, I never denied God existed but I didn't want anything to do with him. We eventually decided to go our separate ways. One of her parting shots was, 'Why don't you do an Alpha course?' She said, 'You're hungry for God without realising it.'

In November 1992, I was working in the City and friends invited me to a Remembrance Day service at Holy Trinity Brompton. After that Remembrance Sunday service, I used to turn up at HTB and sit on my own during a Sunday service right at the back near the doors so I could make a quick exit if needs be. It was my secret. Nobody knew I was there. I didn't get that terror that I had felt in the other church – perhaps because it was in a church building. At least HTB looked like a church even if it was a bit wacky.

Looking back, despite appearances, my life was a bit all over the place at the time. I heard about Alpha and decided to do the January course. I was very nervous but I was quite interested. I expected there would be about eight people there. I thought we would sit on an odd assortment of chairs drinking strong tea, eating stale biscuits and having awkward conversations about God.

When I walked in, I was struck by how many people there were. Everyone had what I thought was a plastic smile and was frightfully helpful and I thought, 'You're not going to pull the wool over my eyes.' My fear really was that they were trying to brainwash me and the place was a cult. I didn't eat the food for the first few weeks because I thought it would be drugged and I would wake up in a bedsit in Hampstead with some cross legged guru sitting at the end of my bed saying, 'Thanks for the money. You know you're not going to see your family again and, by the way, your new name is Leonard.'

I used to look at Christians and think, 'There is something not quite right here. You operate in an odd sort of way. You are different, not normal. I'm going to crack it and get to the bottom of it.' I remember one evening thinking, 'I wonder if they've got funny little chips in their brains or something?' It was weird. I am not being flippant when I say all this – I genuinely thought it.

My first night in a group was awful. I had been told it would be very relaxed, ('Come and go as you please'; 'if you like it you like it, if you don't you don't'; 'no-one will follow you up and come and bang at your door' and all the rest of it). So I was horrified when they passed a clip-board around and said, 'Just pop your name and address on here.' I thought, 'I am not giving them my name and address.' In a blind panic, I decided to give them a false name and address. Then I thought, 'What if I discover that I like the course and then have to explain that I have given them a false surname and address?' So I thought I would compromise and just give them a false surname. That way I would at least get any of the information that they sent me. Thankfully, the group leader sensed my unease and said we didn't have to write anything if we didn't want to. I thought the people in my group were smug, too nice to be true, geeky, over friendly ... I was very cautious. However, there was a very nice guy in the group who was coming from the same sort of place as me. He was a doctor who used to arrive on his motorbike and seemed fairly normal. We used to howl with laughter at the people there and what they believed. We just thought everyone was naive or strange or both.

In hindsight the Holy Spirit was working big time. On the first night Nicky Gumbel spoke I was struck about what he said about Jesus being a historical figure. I had never thought about that before. Even though I had been to the tomb in Israel, I never made that connection. I began reading lots of books and, as the weeks went on, Alpha became a significant time for me. One Wednesday night all the tubes were shut because of an IRA bomb alert and I realised that I was going to miss the beginning of the talk. I was on this bus approaching Trafalgar Square and I suddenly realised that I was desperate to get there. That was quite shocking. I suddenly thought, 'Something is not right here. I am changing.' I started eating the food at Alpha after a while but even then I just started with things which I thought would be hard to drug like bread and salad. Soon afterwards though I started eating the meat and stuff.

Prior to the Alpha weekend I arranged to visit Nicky Gumbel at his house. We talked some stuff through for about an hour. I had been really challenged by a lot of the material and was feeling stressed, so we just talked. At the weekend, I shared a room with the guy who was a doctor. After the Saturday morning talk, Nicky said if anyone had any issues that they wanted to discuss with him, he would be available in the afternoon. I went along and said, 'Look, I kind of believe this now. I've got lots of doubts . . . What about this? . . . What about that?'

He said, 'Do you believe that Jesus Christ was the Son of God and that he rose from the dead?'

I said, 'Yes.'

He said, 'Well, you should become a Christian then. If you like, I'll say a prayer and you can repeat it after me.'

So I said, 'OK.'

It was along the lines of, 'Jesus, I recognise you as Lord. Forgive me for the wrong things I have done in my life. I turn away from all the wrongs and mistakes I have made. I ask for your forgiveness and I give my life to you. From now on, I'll follow you.'

I meant it. That was in 1993.

That night, there was an evening of entertainments and we were asked to volunteer to read a poem, sing a song or whatever, if we wanted to. When the time of the performance came, the first on the stage was a Russian concert pianist. When she started playing, I was so glad I hadn't offered to juggle a few oranges. She was just phenomenal, gobsmacking. I must admit, I thought that the whole thing was going to be really cringey. After that, I went to the bar and got drunk with my friend. After saying the prayer with Nicky, I spent the next two or three weeks thinking, 'I wonder if I am a Christian?' Every morning I would look in the mirror because I thought maybe I would look different. Perhaps I would grow that fake smile or get the chip in the head. But I looked just the same. Then after a few months I thought, 'Well I am a Christian. I read the Bible, I follow God.'

During that time I was reading the Bible every day, meeting other Christians and I saw more of the truth of Christ and the compassion of Christ. Before, I had tended to have the classic view of God as a grumpy old sod who sits on a cloud pointing out people's imperfections and mistakes and saying, 'I'm looking forward to putting you on the barbecue.' That kind of stuff. But now I just saw God's kindness.

This was all the beginning of some radical lifestyle changes for me. I was smoking 20 cigarettes a day and drinking heavily when I went out with my mates and getting into all sorts of trouble. But all that stopped over the next couple of years. Becoming a Christian wasn't a quick fix for me (it still isn't!). I know to my friends I was deemed to be less of a good laugh because I didn't do those things. It was a painful time because I lost contact with many of them, but that was the only way I could do it with hindsight. It was the only way I could transform my life. Thankfully, I see them again now. While those things were becoming less important, the things that were becoming more important were my thirst for God and reading the Bible and praying. My thirst for the Bible was unquenchable, embarrassing even.

Now I enjoy presenting Christ to people. When he is presented as he is, he speaks for himself. He doesn't need other people to do that. I have helped out on Alpha many times now and I have seen many lives transformed by Christ. It makes me sad when I see how people outside the church view God. They view him as something he isn't. A caricature. Many view him like I did as a grumpy old man sitting on a cloud who is out to get them, to criticise them, destroy their fun, make them feel guilty, and make them feel ashamed. But the truth is that he imparts life into people's lives bringing freedom, healing and restoration.

Mike Norris is currently studying theology at Wycliffe Hall theological college in Oxford with a view to being ordained into the Church of England in 2001.

7

'I kept thinking, "What am I doing? This is
madness. It goes against the grain." '

The story of Ken Ashton

> *Soon after starting the Alpha course, taxi driver
> Ken Ashton was faced with a dilemma: should he
> declare all his earnings to the taxman? Here he tells
> how his deliberations became the first step towards
> a changed life . . .*

I used to go to an Anglican church with my Dad when
I was very young. He used to get quite involved in
church but it was just a question of what you did on a
Sunday – you dressed up smart and went. My dad was
very, very strict so whatever he said went. You just
did it.

I first met my wife, Eve, at primary school. We both

grew up in Dagenham but had nothing to do with each other until we met up again at the age of 22. We didn't go to church at first, but in 1992 she started going. When she told me she had become a Christian, I said, 'Well, if it makes you happy.'

I didn't mind her going to church because I thought, 'Well, if she goes to church at least she won't give me any grief about being out all day Sunday cycling.' I used to cycle between 50 and 100 miles on a Sunday so I was away for most of the day. Eve used to keep her faith to herself mostly because I was sceptical and a bit arrogant. She knew that I wasn't over interested. I didn't think it was wrong. I thought it was almost like being a member of a club. 'If that's what makes her happy, then fine,' I'd think.

Then in 1996 Eve asked me to go with her and our daughters to Spring Harvest, a Christian holiday week, at Easter. I knew it would mean a lot to her – make her happy – so I said yes. At Spring Harvest I went along to a meeting called 'Agnostics Anonymous' which I thought was quite interesting and I felt the people weren't so bad. I remember someone saying to me, 'God's got a plan for you.' After that my wife asked me to go on an Alpha course at a local church, St Thomas's Dagenham, and I did. At that time I was working in the print industry as a reprographic planner but I had been training to be a cab driver and I'd already done 'The Knowledge'. After the first week of the Alpha course I left my job and became a full-time taxi driver.

Soon afterwards I was at the rank at Liverpool Street Station when a young woman came to my window giving out leaflets for some Christian play. As it happens, I was reading a Bible as that evening I was going to Alpha. We chatted and she said, 'God's got a plan for you. You know that, don't you?'

It had occurred to me that a possible perk of being a taxi driver (this was just my opinion) was that I wouldn't need to declare all my earnings as it was all cash. So I deliberated over only declaring 80 per cent of my takings thinking that I wouldn't get any grief from the Inland Revenue because it would still be a good amount and they would look at it and be none the wiser. These thoughts were being mulled over whilst still attending the Alpha course.

Then I read in the Alpha manual this prayer of commitment to Jesus Christ. One part of the prayer was: 'I turn from everything I know is wrong.' On the next Alpha night, I said to the vicar, 'I think this is as far as I go on this Alpha course because it says in the manual 'I turn from everything I know is wrong' and I know that not declaring all my takings is wrong and I should declare it all. But it's the difference between giving my girls – we have two daughters – a decent holiday or not.'

He said: 'It's your decision. Think about it.'

And for a whole week following that conversation I was having this major battle going on in my head about what I should and shouldn't do. Come the following Tuesday I thought, 'There's not a lot of point continuing this course unless I actually turn round and say I am going to declare all I earn and see where it goes from there.' I knew that was my stumbling block. So I went back to the vicar and I said, 'Look, I'm going to declare

all I earn because I know I can't continue this course
if I don't.'

He said, 'Great. If you do that God will honour you
for that.'

And I said: 'I don't feel particularly honoured. I've
got to say I'm not particularly happy about this.' It felt
as if I was literally throwing money down the drain. I
kept thinking, 'What am I doing? This is just madness.
This goes against the grain.'

The following Saturday, (11 May 1996, FA Cup Final
Day) I was still struggling with the decision I had made
and I said to my wife: 'This is madness. Does that mean
I declare all my tips that people give me? Does that
mean if you give me a fiver I declare that? This business
of cleaning your act up is nonsense because it can't be
done.'

Then she just said two things to me. First she said,
'The devil's really cunning and he'll do anything to stop
you becoming a Christian.'

Then she said, 'God's got a plan for you.'

It was the third time I'd heard someone say; 'God's
got a plan for you.' Suddenly I was totally overcome
by the Spirit of God and just fell in the chair and cried
solidly. During this time my daughter Louise was doing
a puzzle and she didn't even raise an eyebrow – which
was very uncharacteristic of her.

After about five minutes I stopped crying and as I
looked up, I saw Louise putting the last piece in her
jigsaw puzzle. I realised at that moment that the puzzle
of my own life was completed. Jesus was the missing
piece. I knew that the words Eve had said had come
from God and when I suggested this to her, she got a

lump in her throat and said, 'Before speaking I had said a quick prayer: "God give me the words to say." '

I didn't say any particular prayer, but at that point I recognised that I had been put right with God through what Jesus had done for me. How could I deny what had happened? I couldn't possibly turn my back on Jesus for the sake of a few quid. Now I write down everything I earn.

I don't feel in any way that I've lost out financially. Whatever money you earn you find a way of spending it. I am so thankful that God sorted me out in the first week of becoming a full-time cab driver so I didn't have the mess of sorting out owed tax.

When I told my story the following week in Alpha I cried all the way through it. I could just see how good God had been to me. I was desperate to tell the group I had become a Christian. For at least two weeks after that Saturday I was on another planet. There was nothing that was going wrong. I had to pinch myself in the morning that it had happened. I can only parallel it with when you first fall in love with somebody and you can't believe you're still going out with this person.

Jesus Christ has given me a purpose and a direction in life – even though I don't know what it is yet. He has put a new perspective in me. I didn't think of Jesus before. I had heard the stories that he lived, died on the cross and rose from the dead and although I didn't dismiss it I didn't think it was of any importance to me. My outlook on life now has completely changed to what it was three years ago. My wife and I pray with the girls at night and I wish I'd known about God and Jesus when I was their age.

Ken Ashton and his wife Eve moved to Collier Row, Romford, Essex, in 1997 and now attend a local church there, the Church of the Good Shepherd, where Ken is a leader on the Alpha course. 'I thank God for Alpha,' says Ken.

'Mark came back from his counsellor and said, "I have to decide whether I ought to be married to you or not." '

The story of Carolanne and Mark Minashi

Businessman Mark Minashi and his wife Carolanne were going through difficult times in their marriage when Carolanne went on an Alpha course at Holy Trinity Brompton. Mark responded by singing 'Kum by Yah' in a jokey fashion – but soon their lives were turned upside down:

Carolanne's story

My mum and dad got divorced when I was three years old. Two years later my father went to New York and lived there continuously until his death fifteen years later. In all that time, I only saw him about three times so it was quite sad. My elder brother, younger sister and I had quite a nomadic childhood, but wherever we lived Mum took us to church most Sundays. I went through confirmation classes at about the age of 13 with a lovely vicar and used to have these wonderful one-on-one chats with him and I can remember distinctly feeling very close to God for about a year. Sometimes I used to cycle to church on my own to go to services, but it was hard to be part of an adult church at the age of 13. It all just drifted away.

When I was 18 I met Mark and four years later, in 1990, we got married. Our first home was a flat in Watford. Neither of us went to church – it wasn't something that would have occurred to us. Two years later we moved to a tiny village called Chenies in Buckinghamshire and I started looking for ways to get involved in the community. The local parish church was idyllic and as soon as we moved there, I started going to church. Mark would go with me occasionally but more often I would leave him at home on Sunday mornings. In those days, it was a classic Church of England situation with a congregation of 10 people, nine of whom were widowed women over 70. The tenth was me. However, congregation numbers did pick up during our four years there, especially when David, the new vicar, arrived.

I became pregnant with Alexander in 1993 and Mark and I started going to NCT classes with about eight other couples from the area. One of the couples was Jo and Mark Glen and we became friends. We liked them from the beginning. When I found out Jo was a Christian, I was very surprised. She was the first 'born-again' Christian I had ever met who was normal, with a living relationship with God, and happy to talk about it. I remember saying to Mark, 'You'll never guess – they're Christians. They're really into the church.' Jo started talking about something called the Alpha course, an introduction to the Christian faith, which she had done.

Then, within a month, I heard that my sister Melinda had started doing an Alpha course. Melinda was someone who used to go through lots and lots of phases. When Mum told me that Melinda was doing an Alpha course, I thought 'Yeah, another phase' and completely pooh poohed it. But I started noticing changes in Melinda. When I saw her, she seemed much softer and kinder. I remember one occasion when we met for lunch in London around my birthday and she gave me Nicky Gumbel's book. She was just on fire about it, but I thought, 'I'd rather have Clarin's face cream thank you.'

After Alexander was born, Mark and I started going through some really difficult times in our marriage. I loved him, but he had a really dark side to his character – about five per cent of him – with a lot of unfinished business about his childhood and broken dreams. He was training to be an accountant and it was retakes, no money, big pressure and Mark started to get sucked under in a real depression. In the end, he went to counselling, which he found really helpful. But it wasn't easy for me. On one occasion Mark came back from his counsellor and said, 'I have to decide whether I want to be married to you or not. When I've worked that out I'll tell you.'

I was thinking, 'Well, great. What do I do until then?' But as soon as he finished doing the therapy he was less angry and less hostile; things at work started to pick up and our family life got happier.

I continued to attend our local church but when Alexander got to about 18 months old, he naturally started wanting to run up the aisles. I then became increasingly aware of people 'tut-tutting' under their breath. David, the vicar, was fine about it, but there was a hard core that really didn't think it was appropriate. I ended up hating church because Alexander would start struggling and I would try and keep him quiet and he would hate it and I would hate it. So I just stopped going.

When William was born in 1997, I took maternity leave and had seven months off work. Life was suddenly getting hugely complicated because now we had two children and I had a full time job, a nanny and lots of relationships to juggle. By now I was Director of Management Training in Citibank – with responsibility for the training of all the management staff in Europe. My maternity leave was just coming to an end when Melinda sent me details of the next Alpha course at Holy Trinity Brompton. I remember lying in the bath and praying a prayer saying, 'God, if you can make room in my life to go to this course, then I'll go.' I signed up for the course starting in September 1997 and began to organise my life around it. Mark agreed to look after the boys and all went well for the first night.

I had never been to HTB and remember driving along thinking 'I can't believe I am going to a course on Christianity at this church.' I got there and thought, 'I could just go home and they would never know.' But as soon as I drove up, I received an amazing welcome. I really enjoyed the first night. I didn't know a soul, but I didn't mind. I kept going week after week, although I missed two evenings because of my job.

Then I went on the Alpha Weekend in Chichester. Mark was a bit cynical about it and in the weeks beforehand he kept singing, 'Kum by Yah, My Lord' all around the house. He thought I was going to come back playing a guitar and wearing sandals. I was sharing a room with someone called Elspeth Hughes-Penny and at the end of one of the sessions I was telling her about my upbringing – my dad and my first stepfather and about Melinda. Elspeth asked if I would like to pray with her. I said, 'Fine' but wasn't really convinced.

We were in the big meeting room at the front with hundreds of people all around us chatting away. Elspeth just went completely silent for about five minutes. Then she looked at me and said she felt she had been given a 'word of knowledge' from God for me. It was along the lines of God saying to me 'Don't try and carry the world on your shoulders. You don't have to try so hard. You don't. I am here for you . . .' Then there was more which was directly related to my father. As she spoke, I burst into floods of tears. All that pent up hurt that takes you 30 years to bottle up just came out like that. All those feelings of being unwanted and unloved . . . all to do with relationships with my father and my stepfather . . . It all just came out and I knew it was God.

I knew it was God because there were things which

I hadn't told Elspeth which came out when she spoke. For her to have pieced all of that together with such 100 per cent accuracy would have been impossible unless she had been the most perceptive psychiatric analyst, which she isn't. I now knew I mattered to God as he had sent me a very personal and direct message. All the stuff we had been hearing on Alpha up to that time had been intellectual head stuff and I had not been really there with my heart.

Soon after Elspeth's message, Nicky invited us all to say a prayer which we could say with him. It was a prayer to welcome Jesus into our lives and to say sorry for all the things that we had done. As I said the prayer, I had this feeling like a gold Catherine wheel hitting me in the chest and then shooting all down my arms and legs. When I came home I said nothing – but at the end of the course I invited Mark to the Alpha Supper. I thought it would be nice for him to meet all the people that I had been with all this time.

After the pudding, Nicky came up and asked if he could interview me from the front about my experiences on the course. I was panic stricken, but I said yes and Elspeth and I ran into a corner and prayed. Mark didn't know what was going on and just listened while I told everyone how God had changed my life on the course. On the way home, Mark said, 'I don't understand how you could tell everybody else this without telling me.' I said, 'Well, you would have just pooh-poohed it.' That was Christmas 1997.

Mark and I went to a Sunday morning service at HTB early in the New Year and he said, 'Well, I don't mind going once a month but I'm not going to go more than that.' So we started going to HTB in the mornings and it became more frequent. The intellectual quality appealed to Mark. He found it thought-provoking. By the summer we were going most weeks. I was just dying for Mark to do Alpha and I kept praying for him. He finally did it in September 1998.

I now have a living relationship with Jesus and I know that he loves me for what I am. We are bringing the boys up praying with them and talking about Jesus. Our home is alive and it's just wonderful. There is so much kindness and love ... and that's coming from Jesus – not us.

'I would not have described myself as religious in any way ...'

Mark's story

My mother was brought up as a Catholic. In 1958, she went out to the Sudan and it was there that she met my father, who was Jewish. They married there and settled for a while until my mother became pregnant. She then returned to England while my father remained in the Sudan. My brother was christened while my father was still in Africa. When he found out he went ballistic. My mother was adamant that we as a family were not going to become Jewish and my father was adamant that we were not going to become

Catholic or Christian. So that was the end of any religion in our house.

My first time in church was during my military training at Sandhurst. There you have to attend church parade. I thought it was fantastic because it was an hour off from drill, singing some nice songs with nobody shouting at me. However I never thought of it as anything other than time off from the army. About three years later, as I was going to get married and hadn't been christened, I thought I had better do something about it. The padre was a really nice guy, very approachable, and I went around to his house for the talks. I can't honestly say they made a big impression on me. However, I was confirmed. Everyone else was about 13 years old and I was 26! I didn't tell anybody – not my friends or my parents.

When I got married, my father wouldn't go into the church. He just stood around in the churchyard throughout the ceremony. To my knowledge, my father has never been to a synagogue, but he wouldn't enter the doors of a church. I would not have described myself as religious in any way. I just wanted to get married in a church in the same way that 99 per cent of other people like to be married in a church.

My father had always been very independent and very successful. He ran a property and retail business and I had always been brought up to believe that I would take over the business. But that never happened. While the business had been very successful during the 70s and the early to mid 80s, by the late 80s it had all started to go pear shaped. So the great expectation from that side never materialised. I started doing accountancy training.

In the army, I had been in an environment where I was successful and in a position of authority. Once I started my accountancy training, I was back to being at the very bottom. It was a long uphill struggle and it was very difficult for me. I just felt that I was wading through treacle not going anywhere and just sinking in it. I had always had such high hopes, which Carolanne had shared and believed in. The drudgery of this situation, combined with my father's failing business and a breakdown of my relationship with him impacted our personal relationship. Carolanne felt let down by having to go back to work after having Alexander. It was a confrontational, dark time which was very stressful and left me completely depressed. I didn't know what I wanted but was miserable with what I had.

I eventually went to a therapist and started unbottling my tensions and tried to deal with the negative issues that I was burdened with. This lasted for about a year after which both my marriage and my work were thankfully going well.

When Carolanne went on the Alpha course, I thought, 'Well, if that's what she wants to do then fine.' I did think this was an extra commitment that she just didn't need to take on, although I couldn't help noticing how she certainly looked forward to going. I was saying, 'Are you sure you want to go? You're always going to that place. Why bother?' But she was very determined. When Carolanne asked me to the Alpha Supper, I couldn't really refuse. But had I been on a business trip or something then I would have considered it quite convenient!

My first impression of the Alpha Supper was quite disarming. Everyone was so exceptionally nice and welcoming. Then Carolanne was asked to give her testimony and it became clear that this course had had a great life changing impact upon her. I was pleased for her but wanted to leave it at that. However, we did start going to church at HTB once a month – and then once a week.

I found the talks very thought provoking and I remembered them afterwards. I also liked the informality. That summer, there were upheavals at my work and I was made redundant. I ended up serving out my notice at home on 'garden leave', which made it easy to attend Alpha on Wednesday nights. During the course I started my new job which began the day my garden leave finished, which I now believe was due to God's perfect timing.

The first night of Alpha felt like freshers' week at university. I was quite overwhelmed by how many people were there – well over 600 people upwards. The talk that night was about the factual history of the bible, which was quite interesting because I didn't know any of it. I liked the structure of the course, with the supper, talk and groups. The great thing is that I was able to explore all the Christian basics. As the weeks went on, I found it more and more intellectually stimulating. I had all the classic arguments: how can a God of love allow suffering? Is there an inconsistency with the God of the Old Testament and with the God of the New Testament? I came to a view from an intellectual perspective that some of these areas could never be sufficiently explained. There is a time when you just have to decide whether you believe.

Without question the most life changing event for me was the Holy Spirit weekend in Chichester, which I had gone to with quite a bit of anticipation. On the Saturday, I said a prayer of repentance to God. I sensed that I was repenting for all that had happened in my life which I wished had gone another way and being cleansed of that and being able to move forward. I was very conscious that Jesus died for my sins and that I was now forgiven.

During the Saturday evening Nicky asked for the Holy Spirit to come. Tom Adam, who was my group leader, asked if I wanted him to pray with me. I indicated that I did and he prayed for the Holy Spirit to come. When Tom prayed, I felt a physical force like I was being filled with a powerful wind. My mouth, my lungs, my chest, seemed to be being inflated continually and very powerfully. From a spiritual sense I would say it was like the supernatural kiss of life. It was the ultimate in artificial resuscitation. It was absolutely amazing. I just know it was God. It seemed to go on and on and on and on. It was exhausting.

I thought, 'There is no way I am going to be able to come out of this.' It didn't feel as if I was breathing. But I was strongly aware of God's presence with me. One of the things that Tom Adam prayed at this time was, 'Now, God, let him be the man you made him to be.' That was a very far-reaching insight and meant a lot to me.

Now there is a very big part for God to play in our

lives that never existed before. I never really thought of Jesus before but now I fundamentally believe in the existence of Jesus Christ, the fact that Jesus came to us, lived and died, rose from the dead and lives with us today through the Holy Spirit. I didn't even understand that before – let alone believe it.

My mother, brother and younger sister came to the Alpha Supper, which was great. I am very grateful to them for coming to support me. No one knows you like your own family and they have noticed the change in me since. I have become unburdened and wholly confident in my faith. Alpha has been life changing for me. My one regret is that I didn't do the course with Carolanne, but at that time I felt I wasn't ready. I now know that had I done Alpha I would have been ready. I didn't need to prepare. Alpha does that for you.

Mark and Carolanne Minashi remain members of Holy Trinity Brompton where they are members of a church home group. In 1999, their third child, Natasha, was born. Carolanne says, 'We have continued to grow in our relationship with God and, through that, have also grown much closer together. God has moved in such power in our lives.'

8

'I remember thinking, "If I make generally supportive noises, then she will go off and have an abortion and that will suit me." '

The story of Jonathan Jeffes

> *As a helicopter pilot working in different 'hot spots' around the world, Jonathan Jeffes felt only relief when his pregnant girlfriend told him she was going to have an abortion. Then, some years later, he became a Christian and he felt God speak to him . . .*

My mum and dad never went to church. I was sent to a high church school, where we had to go, but once I left school I never went except for weddings and funerals. To be honest I never really thought about it at all. I would have said there was a God, but more along the lines of a New Age or Hindu model – everything being part of God. I went to university but dropped out to train as a helicopter pilot. From the age of 19 I was flying up in the North Sea – from Aberdeen out to the rigs and from the Shetlands out to the rigs. I did that for about three or four years.

A lot of my friends died in helicopter crashes. I was looking through an album the other day and I counted 15 faces of people that I've known and worked with who died. Probably four or five of those were very good friends of mine. We used to get some very, very hairy moments up in the North Sea, but there is always that feeling when accidents happen that somehow if you'd been there it would have been all right.

We used to see the odd 100mph wind. Once I was in my helicopter sitting on the deck of something called a semi-submersible rig, which used to float on the surface of the sea when I saw a freak wave coming which I thought was going to break over us. There was an air-speed indicator and it was blowing 100mph and I just thought, 'Maybe I should just take off – just save the chopper and myself.' But the wave just kind of passed underneath us.

After that, I spent a year in Canada as a bush pilot (meaning you fly where there aren't any roads) supporting trade in timber, mining, minerals, that sort of thing. Then, for three months, I returned to England and worked in London. It was a time when I was leading a very intransigent life – always travelling a lot, so I never, never had a particularly steady girlfriend.

When I did find a girl that I got on well with, we would form a relationship for a few months and then

I would be off again, either abroad or whatever, and we would usually break up. It was at this time that I met this one girl who was very nice. We started sleeping together and she got pregnant. It was a real mistake, because we were using contraception, but I can just remember thinking, 'Well, I don't really want to be part of this.' Then she said immediately, 'Look, I think I'll have an abortion.' I remember thinking, 'Well, that's good. So I don't have to make much of a decision on this. If I make generally supportive noises then she will go off and have an abortion and that will suit me.'

I didn't feel I was right for marriage and she didn't feel she wanted to be a mother. I saw an advert saying 'Abortion Counselling' in *Time Out*, so we phoned the number and arranged to go and see them together. When we got there, they said, 'You can just go ahead – it's fairly routine,' and she was booked into a clinic the following week. I took her there and dropped her off. It was quite nice, with a lady behind a reception desk with a sign saying 'welcome' and everyone in white coats.

I went to pick her up the next day. She was fine – she's quite a tough person. She got into the car and as we drove back I can just remember a very uncomfortable silence. She was quite upset for a few days following the abortion. She cried a couple of times, which was something she never did. She said, 'Oh, it's my body adjusting – going back to not being pregnant.' She didn't seem that fazed by it. About two or three days after the abortion, various thoughts started to creep up on me, like, 'Well, hang on a minute. I could have been a father – I was a father!' These thoughts started to be very unwelcome and very intrusive. I can remember making a very conscious effort to push them down and not think any of those things. It was almost like putting them in a trunk and locking the trunk and saying, 'I don't ever want to think any of those thoughts ever again.'

Our relationship broke up, partly because I was travelling but partly also because I wanted to get away from her. I went on to meet her a few years afterwards – we stayed friends. I think subsequently she was much more deeply affected by it than I had realised at the time, or, I think, than she had realised at the time. Then I went to Africa for two years, where I had a really wonderful time. While I was there, we surveyed the Kalahari, in Botswana, for diamonds and we found the world's second largest diamond mine. It was a very exciting time. Then I moved back to England and had a job working for the Forestry Commission, spreading fertiliser, for five or six years.

During that time, in 1985, I paid a visit to Paris with a friend of mine. We had separated and had arranged to meet outside the Louvre. I got there about an hour early and decided to go into the Louvre and have a look around. There was an exhibition of seventeenth century Italian painting there and on one of the highest floors, I came across a painting which really struck me. It was a painting of the resurrection, with Jesus standing outside his tomb. It was a slightly ghostly picture and Jesus looked rather pale – almost as if it were a dead body standing there. As I looked, I thought, 'You know, that it how Jesus would have appeared to somebody looking at him the day after his crucifixion. If you had seen somebody crucified in front of you and saw them again the next day, you would just be unable to take it in.' I suddenly thought, 'The guy who painted that picture – he really believed in it. It wasn't a story to him.' Then I suddenly thought, 'Wow! What if it really is true? What if this really happened? What if Jesus really did rise again from the dead?'

As I thought that, Jesus appeared to me in the picture and suddenly it was as if I was standing there before Jesus. And I kind of looked at Jesus and Jesus looked at me. And you may think, 'Well, what a lovely thing – how lovely to stand before Jesus.' But it wasn't lovely at all. It was a very frightening thing, because Jesus looked at me and he had eyes of fire and I felt that he was showing me that I was going to hell. Then he gave me a picture of what hell looked like and what came to my mind, very specifically, as I looked at Jesus, was, 'You have the blood of your child on your hands.'

As I was looking at this image, and these things were going through my mind, there was like a tingling below my forehead and I felt like I wanted to sneeze. And I sneezed and I got my handkerchief out. Then something very strange happened: this one very large drop of blood came out of my nose on to the handkerchief that was on my hand. And I looked at it thinking, 'This is really strange – what is going on here?' I blew my nose and there was no more sign of blood at all.

Then everything just went back to normal and the painting was a painting and I was standing in the Louvre in Paris, looking at this drop of blood on the handkerchief on my hand. I just remember thinking, 'I just want to get out of here,' so I turned and I ran out of the room. I met my friend and we went for a drink. As we sat there, he said, 'What's the matter with you? You look like you've seen a ghost!'

For many years after that, from about 1985 to 1992, I was always on the look-out to see if I could find a church. But I never found anywhere where I felt comfortable. I can remember feeling very, very uncomfortable in all the churches actually. I even went through confirmation classes at one stage, but I remember thinking, 'I really don't understand what all this is about.'

Then, in 1992, something happened which was to change everything. I was in a pub called 'The Ship' in Wandsworth when, standing at the bar, I met a guy who was a helicopter pilot and it turned out we knew loads of people in common. He was there with a big gang of people and said, 'Oh, come and meet the gang.' He introduced me round and I got chatting to one of the women in the party, whose name was Victoria. Somehow the conversation came round to God and she just said, 'Oh, I think you'd find a course that we do at our local church really interesting. The guy who runs it used to be a lawyer so it's all very logical. It's a series of evening talks. Why don't you come along?'

And I thought, 'That sounds quite interesting – I think I'll go to it.' We said good-bye and a little while later, I called this pilot guy up (I knew the company he worked for) and got Victoria's number. So I spoke to her and said, 'You know that course you were talking about. I'd be interested in that.' So she took my address and sent me a form.

Having signed the form, I felt sort of committed, so

I went along. I felt rather uncomfortable with all the people until Nicky Gumbel got up and started speaking. Almost from the word go, I remember thinking, 'Wow! This is something really different. This is really important and it makes absolute sense to me.'

For the first four or five weeks of Alpha my eyes were as big as saucers. I was lapping every single word up and thinking, 'This is it.' Then I went on the weekend, which was really fantastic. I can remember at one point praying a prayer committing my life to Jesus. I just said, 'Jesus, I want to take you into my life now and I want to live with you for the rest of my life.' Then the Holy Spirit just filled me up with love – so much so that I felt I was pumped up like a balloon. I just thought, 'Wow, this is extraordinary.'

Then God spoke to me very clearly. He said, 'You know that thing between you and me – the abortion, that stuff – that's finished. You're forgiven for that and it's completely over.' And I realised then with absolute joy in my heart that I was not going to hell. When I came back from that Alpha weekend I can only say that I felt 'born again'. Then, as we finished the Alpha course, I just knew that everything was true.

After that I started going to church. Then one day I was browsing through the teaching tapes in the book-shop and I saw this one that seemed to jump off the shelf. It said, 'Abortion, by Sandy Millar.' So I took the tape home and listened to it – and I found it fascinating. It wasn't a hectoring, preaching thing. He quoted a bishop who had gone along to a pro-abortion demonstration and had come upon a woman shouting some pro-abortion slogan. And the bishop had said to this woman, 'What do you think God thinks about abortion?' The woman was quiet for a minute and then carried on with her chanting – whatever it was – and Sandy said it became very clear that she had not given the matter any thought.

I was very struck by that story and I remember thinking, 'I haven't given that any thought.' I felt God touch me as I listened and I prayed a prayer saying, 'Oh Lord, is this something you would like me to get interested in?' I felt he said, 'Yes. This is an area in which I am calling you to serve.' I spoke to my pastorate leader, who gave me the telephone number of someone at the Christian organisation CARE. I called up and was put through to someone called Joanna Thompson, who runs Care for Life. Joanna talked to me for a bit and then said, 'Well, why don't you come down and speak to me?'

So I drove down to Basingstoke, where she is, and I spoke to her. She runs a crisis pregnancy centre there and she showed me around the centre and chatted with me for about three hours. She was obviously a very busy person – Care for Life runs over 100 centres around Britain – and I said to her, 'Joanna, you've been very kind spending all this time with me, but why?' And she said, 'We have been running these centres for a long time and you are the first person from central London who has called us up. We've been really praying that there will be a centre in London so I'm giving you time and trying to get you enthusiastic.'

It turned out that she was running a conference on

how to set up a pregnancy crisis centre about a month after that meeting, so I signed up for the conference and went along. There were 100 women, and me, at this conference at the Post House hotel, somewhere up near Warwick.

I thought running a pregnancy crisis centre might be something I should do. I kind of cast myself back into that position and I thought, 'Well, I wish that somebody had challenged all my assumptions then and said, 'Listen, what do you think you are doing? Have you thought about the fact that you are a father? Have you considered going to your girlfriend and saying, 'I really, really would like you to have this baby – if that's what you want to do.' But as I considered where God was leading me, I very much felt him speak to me and say, 'No, that isn't what I want. I don't want you to set up a crisis pregnancy centre. But there is a seminar I would like you to go to.' The seminar was called 'Post-abortion stress and its effects' and it was given by someone called Sheila Clark.

She went on to list, in the seminar, some of the effects of post-abortion stress and she made a state-ment in the seminar where she said that she had never met a woman who had got over her abortion. And I remember thinking, 'Maybe it must be kind of different for men than it is for women, because I have dealt with a lot of that stuff since becoming a Christian and put it behind me.' So I listened politely to what was going on during this seminar.

At lunch afterwards, I sat down next to Sheila Clark on one side, and someone called Margaret O'Hara on the other. We got chatting and then when I mentioned to Margaret O'Hara that I had put my abortion experience behind me, she said, 'If your child had been born, how old would it be today?' I said immediately, 'Twelve and a half years old.' And I can remember the hairs on the back of my neck went up and I stood up and said, 'How did I know that?' It really freaked me out.

It turned out that Margaret O'Hara runs what was then one of the first post-abortion counselling groups. I said to her, 'Margaret, how did I know that, because if you had said to me, "When did your girlfriend have the abortion?" I would not have been able to tell you – not to within two or three years.'

And Margaret gave me her card and said, 'If you want to talk about it, come and talk to me.' So the week following the conference I called her up and she took me through a post-abortion counselling course, which was the most difficult thing I've ever done in my life. It's a very frightening thing because the two thoughts that come are, 'Wow, that was a real child that lost its life' and the other is, 'I killed it.' We prayed a lot and I cried a lot. People say to me now, 'Are you over it now?' and I say, 'Yes, I am over it, but I've never forgotten it.' And to be absolutely honest with you, you never get over it completely.

I met my wife Francesca at Holy Trinity in 1992 and we married three years later. She had been married before and had two children from a previous marriage. We had a service of blessing at HTB and then I moved into the house in Wimbledon where Francesca and her children were. Then we had two children of our own. My step children are Lottie and Henry and they're aged 13 and 11. And then we have Imogen, who is three and a half, and Marcus is two and a half.

Although I gave up flying for a few years I have gone back to it part time and I also run a publishing company part time. As the years went by, I realised that there was a need to create a confidential and safe place where people could talk about abortion within the church.

We set up a post-abortion counselling group to act as a forum where people could come, knowing it would be confidential and that they would be safe. I can't tell you how strong the wall of secrecy on this issue is. People are so terrified of condemnation. I feel that God has called me into the world of post-abortion counselling, not as a political platform, but simply to serve men and women who have been through abortion.

Jonathan and Francesca Jeffes continue to attend Holy Trinity Brompton, where Jonathan runs a regular course for those in need of post-abortion counselling.

'I had a very set view of Christians as really sad people in white socks and sandals.'

The story of Marijke Tapson

When Marijke Tapson's husband Charles announced that he had become a Christian, she was horrified. But as a successful careerwoman, that shock was nothing compared to the devastation she felt when she found she was pregnant with their third child. For many weeks, she seriously considered having an abortion – until God intervened . . .

My father was brought up as a Dutch Calvinist who went to church three times on a Sunday. He felt the most he could expect from his family was for us to go once, and that is what we used to do. We went to the local Anglican church near our home in Hertfordshire but I didn't believe in God and as soon as I could negotiate with my parents, I stopped going

By the time I went to university in London to study speech and language pathology, there were other gods in my life and I enjoyed them. At that age you can party all night and still turn up at lectures in the morning. I shared a flat in an old YWCA building in Devonshire Place with eight other girls and we were always being invited to parties. It was at one of these parties that I met Charles – and about one and a half years later we met up again at another. He invited me out and we began to see quite a bit of each other. When I qualified, I went to work in the Midlands as a speech and language therapist and he began visiting regularly.

We got married quite young and I've often wondered why we did. My mother liked Charles very much, but said I shouldn't marry him because I would make his life hell. We married in May 1979 in our family's village church. My mother never doubted that it would be a traditional wedding and I just thought, 'All right then.'

I quite liked the vicar and I didn't think much about the vows I would be taking. They didn't really mean anything to me. After that, we had a fairly hit and miss marriage. He and I just didn't communicate really. He had a very set view of what a wife should be and I didn't have the same one. He came from an army family and the role you play as an army wife is very different to the one I was used to.

My mother had her own business and was, for her time, quite feminist in her views. I had inherited that and I wasn't prepared to iron his shirts and do all these wifely chores, which caused a lot of angst. Where churchgoing was concerned, however, we were quite similar. Like me, Charles had been brought up as a churchgoer but had fallen away. We didn't go except at Easter and Christmas.

In 1983, my mother died and I had a tremendous reaction to that. I felt I wanted to be free of anything which I associated with her – and that included Charles. In effect, I said, 'I don't want you any more' and we decided to separate. Charles moved out of our home in north London with our two dachshunds to go and live in Teddington. We kept in touch off and on and discovered that we got on quite well when we didn't live together. I stayed working as a speech therapist in north London and Charles continued his work as a surveyor in the City. As the months went past, we met up every now and then.

Despite our separation, Charles's mother was very good at keeping me within the family – and I got on with his sister brilliantly. In fact, I think I probably missed his family more than I missed him. His sister and her husband were living in Germany and one day she sent me some money and said, 'Come for New Year because I don't want you to be on your own.' She knew I didn't have any money. The whole family kept in touch with me and after about 18 months apart, Charles and I decided we'd give it another try.

We sold the house in north London because Charles said he didn't want to live there any more. His work had moved to Victoria, which would have been a pretty horrendous journey from up there. We continued to live fairly separate lives. During working hours, we both had our jobs to go to and, outside work, Charles climbed and cycled – and I didn't if I could possibly help it. I did a lot of amateur dramatics. Both the climbing and the amateur dramatics took up a lot of time.

In 1990 Daniel was born. Charles had decided he would quite like to be a father some time before. As for me, I think if I hadn't had any children I wouldn't be one of those people who thought when they got to 45, 'I wish I had.' I love my children dearly and I have become a much more rounded person since having children but it has been tough for me because I am selfish. Basically I like my own way best and you can't have that with children. I have had to learn the art of compromise and negotiation skills. By the time Daniel was born, I was doing a big job managing a department of around 25 people in Richmond. He was four months old when I went back to work. I had a childminder but it was still quite stressful because you have to say goodbye in the morning and then it is full-time when you come back.

A couple of years later I had a miscarriage after about 12 weeks of pregnancy. I was quite shocked that I didn't really react to it at all. I just thought, 'Oh well.' Lydia was born in 1994 and again I went back to work soon afterwards – although by this time I was in a different job, doing project management for the same health trust. I had a nanny at that point, which made things easier and meant that Daniel could have his friends back to play, which was quite important for him.

Around this time, Charles started to attend a very traditional church in Teddington because he felt that his children ought to have a moral upbringing. Charles got involved in helping the Sunday school and became involved and committed to that church. I used to go occasionally although I didn't really believe in God. I found it a wonderful place to get peace and calm and just spend an hour and a half with nobody bothering me. I could just sit quietly, think about things, pray if I wanted to or just enjoy the music.

In around 1996, Charles's firm of surveyors, Clifford Tee & Gayle were looking at a site near Chelsea Bridge for some clients. Another party interested in the site turned out to be the church of Holy Trinity Brompton and there was some talk of a partnership between the church and this client over the purchase of the site. Charles felt that he needed to investigate this church a bit to see if it was going to be viable to continue along this road.

A surveyor who was working for the church's bid at the time invited him to one of the services at HTB and a group of them went to an evening service. After that, he went a couple more times. He had never seen a church quite like that before and he found it exciting and interesting. He really wanted to find out more, so when he heard about the Alpha course, he decided to go along.

While this was going on, I just thought he was doing it for business. I didn't realise that he really was interested on a personal level – even when he told me he was going on the Alpha course. Perhaps I didn't want to consider that possibility. I almost certainly complained when he said he was going out on Wednesday evenings, but I hadn't really thought that it would affect my life more permanently. I had a very set view of Christians as really sad people in white socks and sandals whom you kept away from. Nevertheless, during Alpha, I did notice that Charles started to be more considerate and thoughtful. He would talk to me about things instead of barking orders at me.

He was often away on weekends, doing climbing or cycling, so I didn't think much of it when he went on the Alpha Weekend. When he came back, we were lying in bed on the Sunday night and he started telling me about it. I was trying to be interested although I was cross about the fact that he had been away while I had had the children. He told me how he had shared a room with a Northerner and I just said, 'Yes, but what did you do on the weekend?'

Then he said, 'I have become a Christian.'

I said 'Oh yes', thinking, 'It will pass.'

Then he told me he had spent most of the weekend crying. I thought, 'That is so weird.'

I tried to let him talk through it but all I wanted to do was get away. I just thought, 'Well, he's one of them now.' To be honest I felt sympathy. I thought, 'Poor man, he can't help it.' Then he told me how he felt and that he was at peace with himself and didn't feel this and he didn't feel that any more. He was totally different.

After that, I began to notice other ways in which he changed. He did more for the children – gave them attention, played with them, which he hadn't really done before. His priorities had always been work, his climbing or his cycling and those hadn't really changed since becoming a father. I am sure I wouldn't have changed either – except that I was forced to because Charles didn't. I am not criticising him in any way but I had accommodated a family because I had to but he hadn't had to. After the Alpha weekend, he made the children more of a priority and spent more time with his family – me and them. So quite soon part of me began to think of his Christianity, 'Well, perhaps I could live with this because there is quite a lot of benefit.'

Charles kept going to the Teddington church in the mornings and started going to HTB in the evenings, so I was soon back to feeling a bit resentful. He persuaded me to go to HTB in the mornings a couple of times. I found the happy clappy music at HTB something of a shock to start with, but I enjoyed the services. There was a tremendous feeling that I had never seen in a church before. I had never seen a packed church that I could recall – and it was very child friendly. They were invited to come to the front and sing with the band and then they had groups and went off quite happily. But I drew the line at attending both HTB and the Teddington church. I said, 'I am not having my whole Sunday in church with lunch in between. I am not doing it.'

Charles gets these tremendous enthusiasms for things which we then get swept along with and I feel I am always accommodating him. It is either 'have a stand up fight' or we have to do it. We had a few stand up fights about Christianity and religion, and in the end I had had enough of it all. I just felt, 'I am not getting into this and it is a load of old rubbish anyway.'

Another thing about Charles is that he likes to be right about things, so I thought, 'I have to get some information on Christianity to use as ammunition to argue with.' I thought, 'The only way to fight this is with information, so I will just have to do an Alpha course. Then I can pooh pooh what he is saying to us.' I looked around for a local course and found one at St Stephen's, Twickenham.

In January 1997, just after booking in for the course, I found out that I was pregnant. It was a terrible shock. I felt that this huge responsibility was falling on me, while Charles was swanning around doing his Christianity and goodness knows what else. I didn't want any more children. I just said, 'I am not having this child' and began to investigate having a termination. Charles was obviously very upset but said that he couldn't stop me and that he would forgive me. He said he couldn't agree with my decision and he had a different viewpoint on it.

Then the pro-life literature started to flood into my house. He was saying, 'Read this – read this.' So I felt quite pressured. At the time he was helping on Alpha courses at HTB and I am sure he mentioned it to people there. It was clearly a huge thing for him. He hadn't been a Christian that long and he believed very deeply in the sanctity of life.

I went ahead with my plan to do the Alpha course at St Stephen's on Tuesday nights and Charles promised me that he would be home every Tuesday in time for me to do it. He kept his word – and it was about the only time that I can recall that he has come home at 6.30pm in order that I could do something at 7pm on a regular basis. That was very unusual and I knew that was only because it was a God thing. If it had been anything else he wouldn't have made the effort. (Though on reflection, greater consideration is definitely one of the ways he has changed since becoming a Christian.)

I was very depressed at the time. I was working so I'd come home, put the children to bed and go to bed and stay there. I was very angry, very angry at God. When I wasn't being angry at God, I was angry with Charles for becoming a Christian. What is more, I was doing contract work and I knew my job was coming to an end. That didn't bother me until I knew I was pregnant and I knew I wouldn't get another job. I thought,

'What am I going to do now? I can't go around looking for a job and be pregnant.'

Charles and I have always been financially independent and effectively we were two separate people. I wanted to maintain my independence because you make a level of commitment when you start to share which I wasn't prepared to make. I felt it represented a loss of control over everything in my life really. I can remember lying in the bath and swearing at God about the fact that I was pregnant and that he had done this to me and how dare he take over my life.

I visited my GP and told her I was thinking of having a termination and said, 'I don't know what to do. I am so depressed I can't think straight. I spend my whole life in bed and I just don't want to get up in the mornings. I don't want to deal with the children. My husband has become a Christian . . .' I just poured all this out.

She gave me 45 minutes and said, 'What do you really want to do about this baby?'

I said, 'I want someone to tell me what to do. I don't know what I want to do, but I don't want to keep it.'

There were lots of reasons why I didn't want to keep it. Mixed in among those reasons was the fact that I didn't want to give in to Charles.

She said, 'Well I think you should terminate it then if that's what you want to do.'

And I said, 'I don't want you to tell me what to do!'

So she said, 'I think you should keep it then.'

And I said, 'I don't want you to tell me that.'

So she said, 'I think you ought to go to a counsellor and work it out for yourself because you obviously don't know what you want to do but you are clearly able to make a decision. Go to a counsellor for six weeks – now.'

So I went and the NHS paid – and it was very helpful.

I went along to the first night of Alpha in early February 1997. There were about 50 people there and they were very welcoming. There were lots of ordinary people there just trying to find out what life was about and to find out about Jesus. The people who ran it were great. It felt very comfortable and you could ask all sorts of questions that you had always wanted to ask. I felt very self-conscious but I enjoyed it very much. I liked the people but then I could console myself with the fact that most of them weren't Christians. I didn't tell a soul at Alpha that I was pregnant because I didn't want their input. I didn't want all these Christians telling me what I ought to be doing.

When the time came for the Alpha Weekend, Charles was thrilled that I was going. I got a lift down to Rye, East Sussex, from an older lady who was in my group at Alpha.

As we drove along, she said to me, 'You've always looked preoccupied when you've been in our group. There is something else in your head that you haven't said yet isn't there?'

I said, 'Oh no.'

She said, 'I think there is. I have lived a long time and I can tell there is.'

So I told her about my pregnancy and said, 'I don't want you to tell anybody because I don't want anyone to know I am thinking of terminating.'

During the talk on the Saturday morning – I can't

remember what was being said – I started crying as I sat quietly at the back. Somebody saw me and came over to pray with me. After that, I cried on and off throughout the weekend. When I had started the course, I had thought I would be able to find flaws in some of the evidence but I was finding it quite difficult to do so. That night, I lay in the bath and thought, 'What am I going to do?' I was thinking about my life and about the baby. By then I was starting to think, 'Well, I will have to keep the baby.' I couldn't really bring myself to have a termination. At the same time, I was thinking, 'This is a mess. I don't know what to do. I am not going to have a job. I'm not going to have any money. I will have to stay at home.'

I just heard the words in my head, 'Trust me' more than once. To start with I thought that I had got myself into such a state that I was hearing things. But I suppose it must have had some impact because, after the meeting the following day, somebody prayed with me and said, 'Do you want to give your life to Jesus?' I had become increasingly convinced by the evidence and I said, 'Yes,' although I remember thinking while she was praying, 'If this doesn't work out I suppose I can always just forget it.'

She took me off into a little room because I was crying so much and I told her I was pregnant and that I'd been toying with the idea of terminating my child. I said I'd come to realise that weekend that I couldn't do it and that I wouldn't be doing it. After that, I can remember bargaining with God, saying, 'OK, I won't terminate it but I want to make sure it's OK and have an amniocentesis [a test for Downs Syndrome].'

I continued, 'If the child is not OK, then we might have to renegotiate this, God, because that's a responsibility I'm not prepared to take and that is beyond the level of trust I can give.'

When I got home, I said to Charles in a casual fashion, 'Oh, I think I probably do believe in Jesus. And I'm not going to terminate the baby.'

But I added, 'I am going to have an amnio and then if the baby's not all right we'll have to think about this again.'

So I booked the amnio, which happened very quickly because by that stage I was at 20 weeks. Within a few days I was lying on the couch at the West Middlesex Hospital. They looked at the baby with the ultrasound and located where they were going to put the needle in. I was aware that with an amniocentesis there is a one per cent chance of miscarriage and as I lay there looking at the baby, I was talking to the registrar and I suddenly heard those words 'Trust me' again – and they were very insistent this time. The words came over and over and over again in my head. And I think at that point I could no longer ignore the fact that these were not just 'me'.

So I said to the doctor, 'Is it too late not to do it now? How would you feel if I didn't?'

He immediately said, 'No, it's not a problem at all. If you choose not to go ahead with it that's your decision and we'll support you whatever you choose.'

I'm sure that either he or his house trainee was a Christian because they bent over backwards to make me feel OK about it. I didn't get any lecture how careful one should be 'at your age' – I was 42 at the time. They just acquiesced.

You know how they describe that tremendous sense of peace you get? Well, I got it and it lasted about a week. It was wonderful. And I just knew that that was God in my life and that he had made that decision. He had given me this child for whatever reason and I'd fought it all the way. Now I'd finally given in and done what he wanted and I never ever worried again that there was going to be something wrong with that baby until the day I was delivering it. In September, Benedict was born and he has been a real joy to us ever since.

After Alpha, I started going regularly to St Stephen's because I liked it. Charles was still crusading at his Teddington church in the mornings and going to HTB in the evenings. He tried to persuade me that my commitment ought to be to his church and I said, 'I'm sorry. I find the church very dry. It's too traditional for me and I want some proper Bible teaching.

'If you want to go there then carry on. I can't stop you. But I don't want to go.'

Then Charles spoke to one of the clergy at HTB, Nicky Lee, and told him about his dilemma because his wife wouldn't support him in going to the church he attended.

And Nicky said, 'You need to worship as a family.' It was quite a difficult decision for Charles to make, but that was when he decided to come with the children and me to St Stephen's.

After Benedict was born, I took my maternity leave but haven't worked since. I felt that God was taking hold of my life but at the time I didn't like it. My whole life changed really because I had to stop working and I didn't feel that bad about it actually. I do wonder what his ultimate purpose is but actually I've enjoyed being at home with Ben. I've done other things because I can't totally be at home, but my self-esteem doesn't come from how much I earn and how powerful I am any more.

I do pray. I don't read my Bible as often as I should but I do read it. Lots of my attitudes have changed. Last year we put an extension on our house to have a bit more space for the children to move in and to breathe around the house. Beforehand I would have compared its size to that of our neighbours, but I honestly don't care any more. Our family life is different too and we do much more as a family. I've always been automatically critical of my children – presumably because I was brought up to achieve. Now I have to stop myself from pointing out their faults because that's not the way to help someone grow. But it all happens gradually. I feel that I am growing inside. Without God, I certainly wouldn't have chosen to grow in some of the ways I've changed.

As for Jesus, I would say that he is now my friend. I don't know him as well as I want to, but he's real. Before I would have said he was some people's fantasy, but not necessarily real. But I know now that he is real.

As for Benedict, he's a lovely and special child. He's a very strong character – but I hope that God's going to channel that for him!

Marijke and Charles Tapson continue to live in Teddington with their family. They have recently taken part in a church 'plant' from St Stephen's.

9

'My temper had ruled my life.'

The story of Luther Blacklock

As professional at the famous Woburn Golf and Country Club, Bedfordshire, Luther Blacklock is one of the country's foremost club professionals. But life has not always been easy. Here he describes how a series of events including the birth of his disabled son Thomas led him to place God at the top of his life's priorities . . .

I was brought up in Reading, Berkshire. When I was 14, we moved to Wales because my dad wanted to start a new business in computers and my mum and sister wanted to keep horses, which they couldn't afford to do in Reading. So we found a cottage in Brecon, mid-Wales. We weren't a Christian family and hardly celebrated the spiritual aspect of Christmas. I had no understanding of what Easter was. I saw Christianity as something to be avoided and certainly an authority against which I would buck. I was cruising for a bruising. I was always arguing with teachers but the RE teacher at school particularly antagonised me. Soon after we moved to Wales, I was introduced to golf by a friend when I was staying with him at his home in Derbyshire during the Easter holidays. From the moment I picked up the clubs, I knew I wanted to do it full time.

It was a perfect excuse for leaving the boarding school I was attending in Hampshire. I found boarding school particularly difficult, although my mum and dad had sacrificed a great deal to send me there. They were greatly frustrated when I found golf. My father said, 'Well, blow you. You can go to the local comprehensive in Brecon.' So I went there and loved it. Not only were there girls there, but I could take the bus home via the local golf club, Cradoc Golf Club.

I became fanatical about golf. It was a drug for me. I was hitting hundreds of balls a day as a youngster – including Christmas Day and Boxing Day. I got my handicap down to around six or eight and then I became an assistant pro at the club when I was 16. My dad was really discouraged because he thought I was throwing away an academic chance. He'd sacrificed a lot for me to go to public school – against his principles – and it seemed as if it hadn't borne any fruit at all.

I fell out with my boss and he fired me and I ended up working in Cheltenham as the senior assistant and continued my apprenticeship. It was at that point, looking back, that I can see the first miraculous thing that God did for me. I had been at this club, Cotswold Hills Golf Club, for a couple of years when my boss promised to take me to a tournament one day. On the morning of the tournament my motorbike didn't start and my boss went without me. I thought about it all day getting angrier and angrier and by the time he came back I was nuclear. He walked into the shop and I just went ballistic. There were a couple of members standing in the shop and he fired me, quite rightly. So now I'd lost my first two jobs as an assistant pro basically just because of my hot-headedness. I phoned a golf pro in Abergavenny, a guy called Philip Worthing, and I asked Philip if he had a job. I didn't tell him I'd just been fired from the last two! So he said, 'That is a funny thing because I phoned *Golf Illustrated* to advertise for a senior assistant last month.

Well, the girl on the phone must have been new because the advertisement ran for a 'Senior Citizen'. He'd had loads of old boys ringing him up with war medals looking for a part time job. In the end, I was the only genuine applicant and even I was capable of getting a job when there was a short-list of one. So I went to Pontypridd Golf Club in South Wales. Philip Worthing was at Abergavenny and I ran this secondary club for him. I got a lovely welcome. Pontypridd is basically a social club with 18 holes of golf attached and I fell amongst all the South Wales people, who are tremendously warm and generous. So I moved back near my old home in Brecon.

One day, a young man called Byron Flynn walked into the shop. Byron is a sports freak who played more golf even than me. He invited me to a party at his home and it was there that I met his cousin Janet and I invited her out. Soon afterwards I discovered that Byron and Janet were Christians. As my friendship with Janet developed I got invited to church and I went along. They were Pentecostal Christians and I remember being struck by the commitment of the praise and of the worship. It just struck me inside that it was just genuine. I thought these people were too straightforward to fake it. They were just so normal. Byron and I became such close friends that Janet and I joined him and his family on holiday on the Gower Peninsula. The girls slept in the caravan and Byron and myself slept under the awning.

On that holiday, I said to Byron, 'I don't know what it is about you people, but there is something different about you.'

He said, 'Well, we know Christ.'

He then offered to lead me in a prayer asking Christ into my life. I said yes and I said this prayer asking Christ to forgive my sin and to set me free. As we prayed, I was physically and tangibly touched by something that felt like a real force hitting my body. It was emotional and I cried. When I woke up the next morning it was all gone. I just couldn't get my head round it and, although my courtship of Janet continued, I didn't go to church any more and just went back to the thing that I knew best which was golf. The compulsion of golf just drove me, like an idiot really. I started buying fast cars and going off to Spain and Portugal. I got myself in a pickle financially.

In 1979, Janet and I got married and in the same

year I was appointed head pro at my old club in Cradoc. Janet is eight or nine years older than me and was 30 when we got married. She had waited for the supposed 'Mr Right', but 'Mr Right' turned out to be me and, as she would say, life was a bowl of cherries until she married me! She is a brilliantly gifted teacher, but she married this nutty golf pro who was totally unfulfilled in his profession.

A year after we were married, she became pregnant. The day Janet went into labour, I was on the golf course. When I got to the hospital in Caerphilly, I found that Janet had had a tough time. She'd had a failed forceps delivery and when I got there I saw the doctor panic and they got me out of the delivery room. They left me out in the corridor and I watched the activity from there. The anaesthetist ran in and after that – it must have been at least half an hour – the midwife came out and said, 'You've got a son.'

I said 'Wonderful. Is he OK?'

The midwife said, 'It's not sorted out yet.'

So she left me there for another 10 or 15 minutes. Eventually they let me into the delivery room. Janet was coming round from the Caesarean section anaesthetic and there was the baby on the delivery trolley. He was a big baby – 25 inches long and 9 lbs, 11 oz – and I can remember his eyes were open. He was a bit bruised and bloodied, but I checked him all over and he had all the bits and pieces that he should. They took Janet and the baby over the mountain to Cardiff to keep them in special care 'as a precaution,' we were told. We had agreed that if it was a boy, I would choose the name and if it was a girl, she would choose. So I got to name him and I named him after the famous golfer Tom Watson. Well, it was a bit inconvenient to me to go and pick Thomas and Janet up from hospital, because I was playing a tournament in Devon. But I did pick them up, stayed in the house for half an hour, and went off to play golf, because that's how much golf was part of my life.

At this point our marriage was crumbling too. I was deeply unhappy and I left home, which obviously seems very callous. I can't believe I did it. But I was so strung out on golf – so mentally stressed out – that I wasn't rational. In the early days it dawned on Janet there was something wrong with Thomas. She was taking him to hospital for post-natal care and at four months her worst fears were confirmed. He was discovered to be brain damaged. It transpired that his ninth chromosome was defective and he would always have the mental age of a baby.

This was Janet's darkest hour because she had waited so long for this baby and she'd now got the double whammy of a crumbling marriage and the news that the baby she'd waited for so long had got this huge brain damage. As a Christian girl, Janet prayed at that point, 'God, if you're there, then just make yourself real to Luther.' It was at that point that I came back. I can't really remember why. I was quite prepared to put the marriage behind me and I'd just cut Thomas out of my mind. Anyway, I came home and we battled on.

Janet kept working and her mother looked after Thomas during the day and I continued chasing the dream getting myself more and more unhappy. The change came about when we had a new minister, Brian Alexander, arrive in the Apostolic Church in the village and he called in to see me for a cup of coffee. I was impressed with that so I went to church that night and Brian prayed for me and said that he felt that the Lord had 'a word' for me. He said, 'Seek first the kingdom of God and all these other things will be added to you.' It was complete gobbledegook intellectually but it just sort of pricked in my heart. I started going to Bible study and did a programme called Evangelism Explosion. Slowly I started to marry intellectually what was happening with what had happened to me in the awning four years earlier.

In church, Brian would ask people to go forward for laying on of hands to receive the Holy Spirit. I went forward three times and nothing happened to me, while old ladies kept speaking in different languages all around me. The third time this happened I stormed out of church and went home, kicked three banisters out of the staircase, and said to God, 'All these ***** Christians on the planet and I'm the one you break your promise to . . .' I was in a purple rage when there was a knock on the door and it was Brian.

Janet said, 'You don't want to see him. He's just too furious.'

Brian said, 'There's nothing that boy could say to me that would offend me at all. It doesn't matter if he hits me and doesn't matter what he calls me.'

Anyway, I sat there in the lounge tight lipped and Brian said, 'Well we know what your problem is don't we?' He meant my temper, the thing that had lost me my first two jobs. He was right. My temper had ruled

THE GOD WHO CHANGES LIVES

my life. But I was far too cross and just swore at him. Three days later I phoned him up and apologised.

I said, 'I couldn't phone you yesterday. I wasn't sorry yesterday, but I am sorry today.' Within half an hour he was round at my house praying for me again. That night I went to church and when I came home, Janet and Thomas and Joan, my mother-in-law, were in bed. I made a cup of coffee and sat by the fire in this Welsh cottage. At that moment, the Holy Spirit came on me and I spoke in tongues for the first time. It was an extraordinary feeling, but it was like being picked up by God and hugged.

Brian said to me later that he felt the reason I'd had such an unhappy time was that golf had become my god and Janet had come second and God had come third. So on the strength of his advice, I resigned my job at Cradoc Golf Club as the club pro in November '83. I just put the knife to golf totally and started studying the Bible and occasionally going around sharing the gospel. But I was now in debt to the tune of £12,000. One night I said to Brian, 'I'm going to be made bankrupt on Wednesday morning.'

He said, 'How much do you owe?'

'About £12,000 or £13,000.'

'Well, how much do you need?' he asked.

I said, 'I need just a couple of grand to keep myself solvent and to give myself time.'

He said 'I've got £2,000.' And £2,000 was all he had. He is a minister who lives off the offerings of 60 people in a small Welsh village. He has three children and a wife. The next day, he went to Cardiff and withdrew his life savings and gave it to me. I was just so touched by that, because I just couldn't believe that anybody would give me so much. He just put his money where his mouth was.

Soon afterwards I got a job working in a sports store in Cardiff and on the fourth Sunday I worked there, Alex Hay, the golf professional at Woburn Golf and Country Club, rang me up and offered me the job as senior professional. I can only describe it as miraculous.

Alex Hay knew me because I had been a pupil of his. He didn't know I was out of golf and certainly not that I was in serious straights. Not only that, but if you had asked me to write on a piece of paper the one person in the world who I would have wanted to work for it would have been Alex Hay, because he was my hero. He's a world class teacher and it would be like understudying Gielgud. It was just a dream come true. I told Brian about the job offer and he said 'Well, it's a lovely thing but we should just wait and confirm definitely that it's of God.'

A couple of weeks later I went to church in Cardiff where an elderly gentleman stood up and spoke these words to the whole church, 'My son, you've been studying all winter and now I'm sending you to a new place where you are to tell people of me.' I just knew that prophecy was for me because I'd been studying all winter and I'd been given this marvellous new job to go to. I just felt that was confirmation. It meant that Janet was able to give up work and look after Thomas full time and also that I was able to work my way out of debt and pay back everybody I owed including my minister and the Customs & Excise and Inland Revenue.

We were welcomed with open arms by a local house church, Milton Keynes Covenant Fellowship, who were wonderful. Pastor David Church and his wife Maureen took us under their wings and just loved us to death and really just enabled us to get our lives back together. I have had the happiest years of my life since our arrival in Woburn.

Before I was a Christian I was afraid of living and afraid of dying. But through the Holy Spirit Jesus has made himself real to me as a person. Where once Jesus was just a misty eyed, historical, hippie-type figure to me I now recognise he is the living Christ. He's a person, a dynamic person, a person who wants abundant life for all of us. All human beings want to do their own thing and I spent 21 years of my life doing my own thing. It was at the point that I could do no more in my own strength that Christ came in and gave me abundant life. If Jesus is the truth, he can't be ignored and if he says that the only way to the Father is through him that's either complete rubbish or the truth and if it's the truth then people need to know about it. It is common sense that people play better golf when they're taught well. Well, people live better lives when they're taught well and if Jesus is the embodiment of God's teaching then we need to take him seriously.

Luther Blacklock is still Club Professional at Woburn and, with Janet and Tom, continues to attend a local church. He says, 'God has met our every need and yet as Tom gets older, bigger and heavier, we will have to trust God even more for his future.'

'The wife of one of Paul's colleagues came to see me at home. She said she had some very bad news.'

The story of Keiko Holmes

Keiko Holmes' Christian faith was challenged when her husband Paul was tragically killed in a plane crash in 1984. She was left to bring up their two young sons alone in a country far from her Japanese homeland. Here she describes how God called her to foster reconciliation between former British Prisoners of War in Japan and the Japanese people – a work which was officially recognised in 1998 when she was awarded the OBE by the Queen.

I became a Christian in 1973 at a Church of England church in Japan. I was interested in Christianity because my husband Paul was such a wonderful person and I wanted to become like him. Paul was British and was living in Japan teaching the English language to Japanese businessmen. He and I met through a Western family for whom I used to baby-sit when I was a student in Tokyo and we married in 1970. In 1979, we came to live in England because life was very difficult for mixed marriage children in those days and we were thinking of their education. We had two sons – Danny who was eight and Christopher who was five. We settled in Croydon where we became fairly regular churchgoers.

In 1983, I went back on a visit to Japan and saw a very close friend of mine who had always argued with me about my Christianity. She had said things like, 'We have many good religions in Japan. Why are you taking up a foreign religion?' But on my visit to see her in 1983 I found that she had become a very strong Christian. She started asking me questions like, 'What does the cross mean to you?' and I couldn't answer. She took me to a Bible camp and there I found out what the cross meant and got to know Jesus Christ. I became more and more fascinated by Jesus.

At this time Paul was a businessman working for a Japanese trading company and he often went overseas on business trips. In 1984, he went on a trip to Bangladesh. One day while he was away, I was reading from the Old Testament on my train to work. It opened at the Book of Job and as I read I saw a vision of a young man falling into a marsh. It was a very strong vision and I can still see it to this day. At that time I was working in the perfumery department of Harrods.

On the Sunday afternoon of that week, the wife of one of Paul's colleagues, who lived next door but one, came to see me at home and told me she had some very bad news. She told me that Paul had been killed in a plane accident while on an internal flight in Bangladesh. I later learnt that the plane had gone down into a marsh. In the days after that, I was in desperation. I didn't want to go on but I sensed Jesus saying to me, 'My grace is sufficient for you. We will work together.'

At that time Sandy Millar [Vicar of Holy Trinity Brompton] was the chaplain to Harrods and used to visit and talk to the staff. I decided to go to Holy Trinity Brompton for a lunch time service in the chapel about one month after Paul's death. I walked in very brave-faced but during the service I just burst into tears. It was then that I got to know Sandy. After the service he came up and spoke to me and then prayed for me. I just cried and cried and I sensed the pain coming out. I started attending a lunchtime Bible group twice a week to which Sandy Millar used to come. After that I gradually started coming to Sunday services at Holy Trinity Brompton.

I attended an Alpha course at the home of Nicky and Sila Lee. It must have been one of the first Alpha courses and there were only around 8 to 10 people at that time. I joined a home group and have very happy memories, particularly one weekend away at Malsh-anger. In around 1986, I started attending churches nearer my home.

Then, in 1993 or 1994, Danny became born again and was completely changed. I was so pleased. It happened through a friend of his who went to a Pentecostal church. I saw some videos of Pentecostal services and thought, 'This is what I have been looking for.' I became more and more fascinated by Jesus and started attending Kensington Temple where they support my work with prayer.

My work with the prisoners of war dates back to 1988 when I went to Japan and visited a large grave of

16 POWs who died in a copper mine five miles from my home. I had visited the grave with Paul many years before, but now it had been completely transformed. There was a beautiful marble stone and a memorial garden. I was so touched by what I saw and strongly felt that I had to find the families of the soldiers who died there. Also I thought I would very much like to meet POWs who had worked there. I prayed about it for a year and after that came to know a prisoner of war who had worked in this copper mine.

He lived in Northumberland and we started writing letters to each other. I sent him some enlarged photos of the memorial and a paper cutting of an article, which showed the former school children, who worked alongside the POWs. After that he came to see me and I went to see him and gradually I met more POWs. I gradually made contact with school children and Japanese miners who the POWs had worked with. Many of the school children were 15 year olds who had been sent to work alongside the POWs during the war. I found these people.

The Army had told them not to communicate with each other, but when the guards were not looking they had given clothes, food and cigarettes to each other and exchanged language lessons and showed photos of each other's families. I began to think that God was calling me to do something in this area but wasn't sure.

In 1991, I went to the British POWs National Annual Conference in the Barbican. At first when they saw me, they wanted to throw me out. They shouted at me. I showed them pictures of the grave and then some people changed their attitude. In the end they sold me a ticket and I went in. When I went in I found the atmosphere very heavy. I felt pain. In the room there was a terribly strong hatred towards the Japanese people. I just sat there and quietly called, 'Jesus, Jesus.' I felt I heard him saying, 'I love them as much as I love you. I died on the cross as much for them as for you.' I was thinking about the Japanese soldiers, who were so cruel and asked God for forgiveness. If only they had known how much God loved them, they could not commit such atrocities. Then I knew that God was assuring me that he loved the Japanese people just as much as the British. I knew that the Lord was urging me to work in helping the process of healing and bringing about reconciliation. I remembered what Jesus said about the time Paul died – He said, 'We will work together.' I understood what he meant. Then I knew that I had to carry on.

In 1992, I started fund-raising and went to Japanese companies asking for help in sending British prisoners of war to Japan. It was slow going but in the end a Japanese national newspaper took it up and money came in at the last moment. Twenty eight people travelled to the mine including two wives.

We had a memorial service there together with guards, (including the interpreter who had been there during the war) and miners and students. One of the POWs was a retired Canon of York Minster and there were two Japanese bishops there. Many of the POWs said their anger was washed away. There were lots of receptions and the Japanese were so eager to receive them.

Many of these men had worked on the Thai-Burma

railway before being sent to the mine. On the mine it was not quite so bad as it had been on the railway. They were given hats, clothes and blankets. Nevertheless, one was very bitter. He was so angry. He said, 'I am going to see if this grave is really there.' My friend and I prayed for him personally and by the end he was the most changed person of all. They realised that the Japanese people were really no different. They said that their nightmares stopped and they were happier people. They said their war ended then.

Since then I have organised regular trips from Britain to Japan and from Japan to Britain. I take any of the Far East POWs (FEPOWs) who were in Japan or the Far Eastern countries and they are mixed between those who worked on the mine and those on the Thai-Burma railway. God is healing them by their meeting Japanese people. We arrange for them to stay with Japanese people overnight, something that they often don't want to do to start with but afterwards they are always so glad they did.

On our trip in March 1998, a Japanese soldier stood up before them all and admitted what he had done. He apologised publicly and personally. One POW said it had been very difficult but he had gone up and shook hands. Afterwards he said, 'This is the best thing that has ever happened to me.' That man had originally said, 'No way' when I had suggested a trip to Japan. It took a long time for him to decide to go. When we go on our trips we visit many different places in Japan. We go to Hiroshima and Nagasaki and hold memorial services there. We also go to the Yokohama British Commonwealth War Cemetery which is often a very important event for the POWs. We have Christian services all over the place.

Just before our trip in March 1998 I received a letter which said that I was to be awarded the OBE. I was very surprised. They wanted to know what day I could make to receive it. At the time I was very busy preparing for the pilgrimage and I put the letter aside. Later the Foreign Office rang me and asked which day I would be available. They also said they wanted to invite POWs and asked me to choose who. I said I couldn't possibly choose. Then they suggested taking all the POWs who were going to Japan in March. Nineteen POWs, including their families, were due to come with me and most of them came to Windsor Castle. My two sons Danny and Christopher also came with me. It lasted from 12 noon until 12.45pm which seemed a very long time. For the first 15 minutes it was just my sons and me with the Queen and the Duke. The Queen was so nice. She was smiling and said I was doing wonderful work. She said she knew that at the beginning the POWs hadn't listened to me so she knew a lot about me. She asked me how it had all started and I told her about God. She was very nice and wished me continued success.

The Windsor Castle people said afterwards that it was very rare for the Queen to be so relaxed. Later she spoke for a long time to all the POWs. The Duke was very kind and very friendly as well. I still can't get over that they made all these arrangements just for me and POWs. It was so overwhelming.

When I saw the trauma in the Barbican Centre I knew that God wanted me to work with him for them.

Now all those who had shouted at me come to monthly luncheon meetings at my house and are all for the work of reconciliation. There are many FEPOW Clubs and many clubs kindly write about me in their newsletters. They are totally changed. In 1998 I got an invitation to Buckingham Palace to attend the Queen's banquet in honour of the Emperor of Japan. I went with my son, Christopher, and the Queen came up and said, 'How lovely to see you again.' I met the Emperor and he said, 'Thank you for looking after so many British POWs.' The Empress also said so many kind things 'from the bottom of her heart.' I sat next to the top man in the Foreign Office and also someone in charge of the Navy. It was very interesting. I also spoke to Tony Blair and Prince Charles and lots of other people I would never have dreamt of meeting.

After that I was invited to attend the return banquet the Emperor held for the Queen at the Victoria and Albert Museum. I was also invited by the Japan Society to a lunch at the Grosvenor House Hotel in honour of the Emperor and I went with Danny to that. I spoke to the Emperor and Empress quite a few times at these occasions. The Emperor had obviously studied facts about me because he said, 'I am very sorry about your husband.' They were both very, very friendly.

Jesus means everything to me. Without Jesus I could not live even a day. When Paul died, God gave me the verse from John 15: 'I am the vine; you are the branches.' As long as I am in this vine, I am safe. If I go away then I am finished. Every morning when I wake up Jesus is there. All the time Jesus is with me. I was one of a family with five children. My two sisters and two brothers paired up and I always felt that I wanted a brother. When I married Paul I felt that he was that brother. Now I feel that Jesus himself is like my brother. I am so grateful to Paul, who led me to the Lord Jesus Christ. Jesus is now my brother, my God and my Saviour. He will always protect me. He is my life.

Keiko Holmes remains a member of Kensington Temple church and continues her work with Agape. In March 2000, she was invited to visit Empress Michiko at the Imperial Palace in Tokyo, where they spoke for more than an hour about Agape's work of reconciliation.

10

'We were spiralling down, out of control.'

The story of Billy and Debbie Bell

> *Billy Bell and his wife Debbie, of Belfast, Northern*
> *Ireland, were close to separation after six years of*
> *marriage. Billy was drinking more and more in the*
> *evenings and was shouting at his wife and young*
> *son, Sam, regularly. Debbie was unable to come to*
> *terms with the death of her mother. Then some*
> *friends recommended they do the Alpha course.*
> *This is what happened . . .*

Billy's story

My mum was Catholic and my Dad was Protestant.
They got a lot of flak from their relative families
for marrying each other and neither had much time for

the church. I was born and brought up in a really working class home in the Shankill Road, which is very, very Protestant. There are a lot of good Christian people there but there are also an awful lot who never even bother going anywhere near a church and I was brought up like that. It was a struggle for my parents. I have a brother and two sisters and there was never much money.

My Dad was a builder and he drank a lot, which meant my Mum had to scrimp. Dad would give my mum a certain amount of money a week and she had to get everything out of that, as well as look after the kids and all.

That area of north Belfast contains lots of pockets of really bitter Catholics and really bitter Protestants living side by side. I was beaten up lots of times as a kid because I had to walk to school through a Catholic area and they would be lying in wait to give you a kicking. I never thought about God. I heard it at school and all, but it never really sank in.

After leaving school, I started working in a local supermarket and it was there that I met a sales rep who told me he was leaving his job and that they were looking for someone to replace him. I applied and got the job. Then, six months later, I moved to work for Nestlé, which is where I have worked since 1987.

My Dad drank a lot and my mum was also quite a drinker, so from the age of 16 I would have been downing two or three litre bottles of cider and whatever else I could get my hands on. I now look back on my childhood and I didn't like it. I really didn't like it. It all revolved around drink. My whole household was all revolved around alcohol. As for the Troubles, if you were wise you steered clear. I was asked to join a paramilitary organisation at an early age, but I said no. I think it was because I have family that are Catholics. Every Friday and Saturday night I'd go into town – and that was how I met Debbie. I asked her out almost straight away and then six months later I asked her to move in with me. That was in 1990.

Then one day I visited my parents and found my mum doubled over in pain and my dad putting her into the car to take her to hospital. She never got out of hospital again. She had cancer and died seven months later at the age of 57. It was horrific. I drank a lot when my mum died, particularly at weekends. That's all I would do. I couldn't drink that much during the week because of having to drive the next morning and I was always aware of that. As for my dad, he started drinking very heavily and in March 1994, he came out of a bar, drunk, and walked into the road and a car knocked him down. He died two weeks later from his injuries at the age of 61.

When Dad died, I decided I was never ever going to get hurt like this again and I made a conscious decision to harden myself and not let myself be close to anybody. I got to the stage where I became a really horrible person. I really did. I was really, really bad tempered and not good fun to be around – and that's the truth. If I said something and didn't get the right response I would just blow – completely blow it out of all proportion. My dad had been very like that – very short tempered.

Our young son Sam had come along at this stage

and although he was only a toddler I was shouting at him too. By this time, my drinking had progressed from cider to wine and I would finish two or three bottles of wine a night. Debbie didn't know how to handle my parents' deaths, so I remember thinking when her mum died, 'Debbie wasn't much help to me when my parents died, so why should I be any help to her?' It was very nasty of me. It meant Debbie didn't have a husband who she could share her feelings with and she had to go through a lot of this on her own. Then I started blaming her because the whole family was just breaking apart. It was so bad that if I'd had somewhere to go I would have left. But I didn't have anywhere to go. It was a downward spiral. We were spiralling down, out of control. There was only one outcome – separation.

In January 1999, Debbie's physiotherapist, Mrs Gunning, gave Debbie a tape of her son giving a talk called 'Two Kingdoms'. He is an evangelist and Mrs Gunning suggested we listen to it. Debbie gave it to me and I put it on in the car as I was driving. And this fellow said, basically, 'If you lived on the Irish border, you would have to say 'I live in Northern Ireland' or 'I live in southern Ireland'. You couldn't tell the authorities, 'Well, I sort of live in both.' You have to make a decision. You have to live on one side or the other.' He said, 'It's the same in the spiritual world. You can't live on the border. Do you live in the kingdom of light or do you live in the kingdom of darkness?' And I remember thinking for the first time in my life, 'I am living in the kingdom of darkness.' But I didn't quite know what to do.

I knew I loved Debbie, but even when we went away together to Paris, the city of romance, in March 1999, it was still a shambles. So what was wrong? I started saying, 'I can't be this unhappy all the time. There has got to be more to life than this.' I had a decent job, we had enough money, we had a fine house, we had a son, I had a beautiful wife. What was my problem? Why was I so unhappy? I couldn't put my finger on it.

We saw our Christian friends Lynas and Marie Lacey in the supermarket on our return from Paris. They said, 'We're not trying to hassle you people. We just love you and we see what's happening. And we know how much Jesus could fix your lives.' And I just stared at them and thought, 'They're right.' So we went to the church and I looked around and thought, 'There's such a lightness about these people and no heaviness. I want my life to be like that.'

We were invited to an Alpha supper, where we heard one guy in particular who spoke about what had happened to him on the previous Alpha course. He had been quite a drinker too and was about my age with a young son of about Sam's age. He spoke of how God and Jesus had transformed his life, and he was so happy. Those were the words I wanted to hear. I just wanted hope, happiness, love – all the things that were missing from our lives. So by the time the Alpha course began, I was the first in the queue.

From the first night, when the group leader asked me who I was, I just spilled out a whole lot of garbage about my life. I was just dead honest and said, 'I'm here because I want to know about Jesus. I want to know how he died for me and what it's all about.' I asked lots of questions and by the end of the third week I said to Debbie, 'Debbie, I want to become a Christian tonight.' So that is what I did. I just sat on the bed and said, 'Lord, I've lived in this world for 32 years without you and I've just heard about you for the first time. I'm so, so sorry for all the things I've done in my life. I need you in my life because I'm going over without you.'

As the weeks went on, I started to forgive everyone who had ever hurt me in my life and I felt the bitterness just being lifted from my heart. It just went. And Peter and Beryl, our group leaders, were getting excited because they could see us changing and we could feel the change. God was in our hearts. I was so looking forward to the Alpha Weekend because I'd heard about all this gift of tongues. But when the afternoon came and we were all prayed for, I felt absolutely nothing. I was so disappointed. Debbie was crying a lot and when we got to bed, we both said, 'I think we'll go home in the morning.' Then, that night, in my dream I spoke in tongues. I woke up at 6am and, unlike most dreams, I could remember it. I could even remember the words. Immediately, I turned to Debbie and said, 'Debbie, I'm not giving up on this. There's no way.'

I sat up straight and said, 'Look, it doesn't matter about tongues. It's, like, Jesus. He loves us.' They had mentioned the baptisms the night before and I said, 'I'm going down and I'm going to get baptised.' I so wanted her to be baptised with me and said, 'Debbie you've got to do this.'

She said, 'I'm not doing it.'

I went, 'Please, please.'

And Debbie said, 'No.'

I went straight downstairs. It was 6.15am and there, waiting for me, was our group leader Peter Quigley. He said, 'I knew you were coming down here this morning because we were praying for you and God told me.'

And I said, 'Peter, Debbie won't come.'

He said, 'I'll get Beryl to talk to her.' That's his wife.

The baptisms were set for 8am and there I was down on the beach walking into the water when Peter shouted, 'Billy!'

I turned round and he said, 'Wait, there's somebody here.'

And Debbie was there. She ran into the water next to me. We got baptised together and that just made it perfect. When we came up out of the water, we were so excited.

What God has done in my life is amazing. I was the most un-gentle person you've ever met and he's just come into my life and turned it around. Patience wasn't a virtue for me – I didn't have it – but now I seem to have it in spades. I find I rarely get angry. I don't raise my voice. I couldn't possibly have made that much of a change in myself on my own. There is only one person responsible: Jesus. It's Jesus, Jesus, Jesus. I have even lost two stone since last year because I've virtually stopped drinking. I only drink socially now – just the odd beer or glass of wine. We've joined a local gym and I am fit now. I've never been fit in my life! I've read all the New Testament – and I can't get enough of the Bible now.

When I am driving along in the car, I sometimes just

turn the radio off and pray to the Lord. I thank him continually for saving me. I thank him for what he's done in my life and hand over any worries I may have. I ask him to guide me and I ask him to forgive my sins, of which there are many. Now I try not to do anything that's going to annoy my Lord, because I love him with all my heart and soul. I always thought Christianity was about what you couldn't do – 'you can't drink,' 'you can't do this,' you know – but it's not. It's about what you can do.

After becoming a Christian, Billy experienced an extra-ordinary answer to one of his prayers. Here he tells the brief story:

I had lost contact with all my family but when I became a Christian I contacted them all again. I have a sister, Sharon, who's an alcoholic. I went to see her in a rehab centre. She hadn't seen her kids for about a year because they were with their father and they had lost touch. I talked to her about what God had done in my life and she was really happy for me.

She said to me, 'Do you think you could bring the kids down to see me?'

And I said, 'Well, where are they living?'

She said, 'I don't know.'

So I looked at her and said, 'Sharon, I haven't seen Charlie, your partner, in five years. How would I know where to find your children?'

She said, 'Please try.'

That was in Newry, 60 miles from Belfast, and I was

driving back home and I prayed and said, 'Lord, would you just help me here?'

That was on a Sunday. The following day I was driving along a dual carriageway in Belfast when I stopped at a red light. A car pulled up alongside me and I looked inside. It was Charlie, Sharon's partner. I hadn't seen him in five years. I flagged him over and said, 'Hi, how are you?' I told him Sharon was in a rehab centre and wanted to see the children.

I said, 'Do you think you would let me take the children down?'

He said, 'Oh, yes. They miss they're mum. No problem.' So the next Sunday, I turned up at the rehab centre with the children and Sharon just couldn't believe it. She just couldn't.

'Our relationship was coming to an end ... and I couldn't fix it and neither could Billy.'

Debbie's story

I went to Sunday School occasionally when I was small but otherwise I had no Christian background. I wasn't baptised as a child and my parents never went to church – not even at Christmas. When I left school, I went into finance work and met Billy in 1990 when I was 21. I was out at a disco bar with some girls from work and someone just introduced us. We got talking and from there started dating. We moved in together shortly after that and then lived together for a couple of years. A couple of years later we got engaged. He had no church background either so we thought it would be nice to go abroad to get married. We went to Mauritius – just the two of us – and were married in a garden by one of the local registrars on 16 September, 1992. Sam was then born in July 1995.

In 1996 my mum died at the age of 66. It was completely unexpected and I sort of fell to pieces after that. Things started to go downhill. I was constantly crying and didn't really want to talk about it. Billy found it very difficult. At that time, I remember crying out to God in the bathroom, saying, 'I'm so unhappy. How could I be this sad? Why am I so lonely?' Shortly after that, I pulled a muscle in my back and was in a lot of pain. So I looked up *Yellow Pages* and found a physiotherapist in our area called Rosemary Gunning. When I went to her house for the appointment, I remember seeing a poster which said something about loving God and so I remember just thinking she must be a Christian.

I started going twice a week and she was very, very lovely and easy to talk to. One day she talked to me about her mother dying and said she and her family had been able to celebrate it because, she said, 'We are Christians and we know she has gone to be with God.' I found that a bit strange but I questioned her quite a bit and started speaking a little about my mum, which I hadn't done with anyone at that time before. I hadn't opened up at all to anyone.

From then on things about my life began flooding out to her and I told her how things were a bit flat between Billy and me. And she said, 'You shouldn't be

THE GOD WHO CHANGES LIVES

going through this. God has a plan for you.' Then she added, 'God is just like your daddy. He loves you so much and has a plan for your life.' Those words really stuck with me. Then she started telling me about her church and mentioned the Alpha course, which she said was an opportunity to learn the basics about God in relaxed surroundings with a group of other similar people. I thought, 'Well, I suppose that makes sense because I don't really know anything about this.'

Around that time, Mrs Gunning gave me a tape of a talk called 'Two Kingdoms' delivered by her son, who is an evangelist. I gave it to Billy and he listened to it in his car. He said he had found it very interesting. At around that time, Mrs Gunning gave me the copy of something called the 'Sinner's Prayer' and suggested I might like to say it for myself. It was basically a prayer saying sorry for the life I had led and then asking Jesus into my life. One night I went upstairs to my room, sat down on the floor and said the prayer. I did feel excited after I said it but nothing too much then happened.

At the same time as this was going on, some friends of Billy's, Lynas and Marie Lacey, had started talking to Billy about going to church. It was the same church as Rosemary Gunning – the Christian Fellowship Church in Strandtown. So Billy, Sam and I went to the church. There were about 400 people there and it was very lively. It was around Easter time and I remember them talking about Jesus dying and God raising him again. I remember noticing the closeness everybody had, but I felt like a stranger when I was there.

Soon after that, on my thirtieth birthday – 19 March, 1999 – Billy and I went to Paris for what we planned to be a romantic weekend. We got Sam minded and went off, but throughout the weekend we couldn't talk to one another. I cried a lot about my mother and Billy just couldn't cope. So I just shut myself off and the barriers started building up. It was the most dreadful time. Our relationship was coming to an end. Everything was just going rapidly downhill and I couldn't fix it – and neither could Billy.

On our first day back from Paris, we went shopping and bumped into the Laceys. They cracked a few jokes with us and then said, 'Look, we love you guys and we want to see your life working out. Why don't you come down to the church again?' So we went back to the church on the following Sunday, where they announced that a new Alpha course was starting where you 'can ask whatever questions you like about Christianity.' Marie and Lynas said afterwards, 'We've got you two tickets to the Alpha supper. Let's go.'

We thought, 'OK, we're on for that.'

When we got to the Alpha supper, I was very nervous, but by the end we were both sure we wanted to do Alpha. Life couldn't get any worse for us, so this had to be something good.

The course itself took place at the home of a couple called Peter and Beryl Quigley. There were about 10 or 12 of us in their front room and after the meal, they said they were going to put on a video tape. I thought, 'Oh no. I really don't want to listen to a video tape. It's going to be boring.' But it wasn't boring. It was really interesting. After that first night of Alpha, Billy and I started to get really excited. We were the first there. I can't tell you what the excitement was like. We were like two children saying, 'This is brilliant.'

People began to notice a change in me at work and they would say, 'You look different to me. What's going on?' I was on such a high – so excited. I literally wanted to dance on the tables. By the time of the Alpha weekend, things were already getting better between us. But I was worried about the weekend and I told myself, 'The one thing I'm not definitely not talking about is Mummy dying.'

There were about 40 people on the weekend because we joined together with other Alpha groups. On the Saturday afternoon of the weekend, there was a talk about the Holy Spirit and the speaker said, 'If there is anyone who wants us to pray with them, do move towards the back.' So I went to the back and a couple of people started praying with me. As they prayed, I felt a deep, deep cry coming from the pit of my stomach. I just started crying and I cried and cried for most of the time. I actually cried for most of the weekend after that. After all the happiness I had experienced through the course, I wasn't sure I liked it.

On the Sunday morning, I really wanted to go home because I was crying and sobbing so much. By that time, Billy had decided to get baptised in the sea with a group of other people there. He wanted me to get baptised with him, but I didn't really feel comfortable about it. I wasn't in great form because of all the crying. But then, as I walked down to the beach, I suddenly got a sort of picture in my head that Jesus was out there baptising people and that I wanted to be one of those people. At that moment I knew instantly that I wanted to be baptised. I nearly ran into the sea after that, wearing just my jeans and flip-flops and a T-shirt. Billy was already there and the two of us were baptised together. The sea was freezing but as we came up, we both went like, 'Yeah.' Everybody was cheering and waiting for us. It was great. I did cry, mind, after I came back!

After that, our marriage began to mend, big time. It felt like we had just started all over again and all those years before were just nothing. I felt like I hadn't lived. I felt like I was opening my eyes for the very first time, seeing everything new and fresh. As for Billy, he was like a new person – more loving, caring. I just fell in love with him all over again. I really did. We didn't want Alpha to end really. The group had a real closeness so after we finished the course, we all studied Philippians together and we became a small group within the church.

Before doing the course, I felt that I'd done without love for so long that I couldn't give love out and I didn't want to receive it from anyone. After becoming a Christian, I felt, 'I can't take any more love. I'm going to burst if I take any more love.' Now I talk to God all the time. I pray, 'Lord,' 'Father God,' or sometimes just, 'Dad' and ask for help with anything I am struggling with. It's like he's always there. Beforehand, I would never have picked up a Bible. It didn't mean anything to me. Now it means something to me because I can relate it to things that are happening. I wish I could give you the words to describe how I feel now. If it wasn't for Jesus and what he went through for us on the cross, then I wouldn't be here living this life now.

Billy and Debbie Bell remain members of the Christian Fellowship Church in Strandtown, Belfast, where they are on the team which organises the church Alpha courses.

If you are interested in finding out more about the Christian faith and would like to be put in touch with your nearest Alpha course, please contact:

The Alpha Office, Holy Trinity Brompton, Brompton Road, London SW7 1JA
Tel: 020 7581 8255 Fax: 020 7584 8536
Email: alpha.office@htb.org.uk
Website: www.alpha.org.uk

The God Who Changes Lives
Volume One & Two

Edited by Mark Elsdon-Dew

Does God act in people's lives today?

Two volumes of stories from people whose lives have been dramatically touched by an encounter with God. Some tell of restored relationships; others how they have been given strength in the midst of pain.

This is a book for anyone interested in whether God is there – and what he can do.

Questions of Life by Nicky Gumbel

What is the point of life?
What happens when we die?
Is forgiveness possible?
Who is Jesus?
What relevance does he have for our lives today?

In fifteen compelling chapters Nicky Gumbel tackles
the answers to these and other key questions,
pointing the way to an authentic Christianity that is
exciting and relevant to today's world.

'*Questions of Life* is a sympathetic, fascinating and
immensely readable introduction to Jesus Christ –
still the most attractive and captivating person that it
is possible to know. Nicky Gumbel's informed
approach ensures that the search for truth fully
engages our minds as well as our hearts.'

– From the foreword by
SANDY MILLAR

Why Jesus? by Nicky Gumbel

Many people today are puzzled about Jesus.

Why is there so much interest in a person born nearly 2,000 years ago?
Why are so many people excited about Jesus?
Why do we need him? Why did he come? Why did he die?
Why should anyone bother to find out?

Nicky Gumbel tackles these issues in *Why Jesus?* a challenging, short presentation of Jesus Christ.

Nicky Gumbel practised as a barrister and is now ordained and on the staff of Holy Trinity Brompton, London.

These publications are available from your local Christian bookshop, or through the Alpha hotline.

Alpha hotline for telephone orders:
0845 758 1278 (all calls at local rates)

To order from overseas
Tel: +44 1228 512512
Fax: +44 1228 514949